14.23-2

HOUSE OF DRACULA

MagicImage Filmbooks
Presents

HOUSE OF DRACULA

(The Original Shooting Script)

Edited
by
Philip Riley

Interview with Jane Adams

Production Background
by
Gregory Wm. Mank

Foreward by Paul Malvern

Introduction by John Carradine

MagicImage
FILMBOOKS

UNIVERSAL FILMSCRIPTS SERIES
CLASSIC HORROR FILMS - VOLUME 16

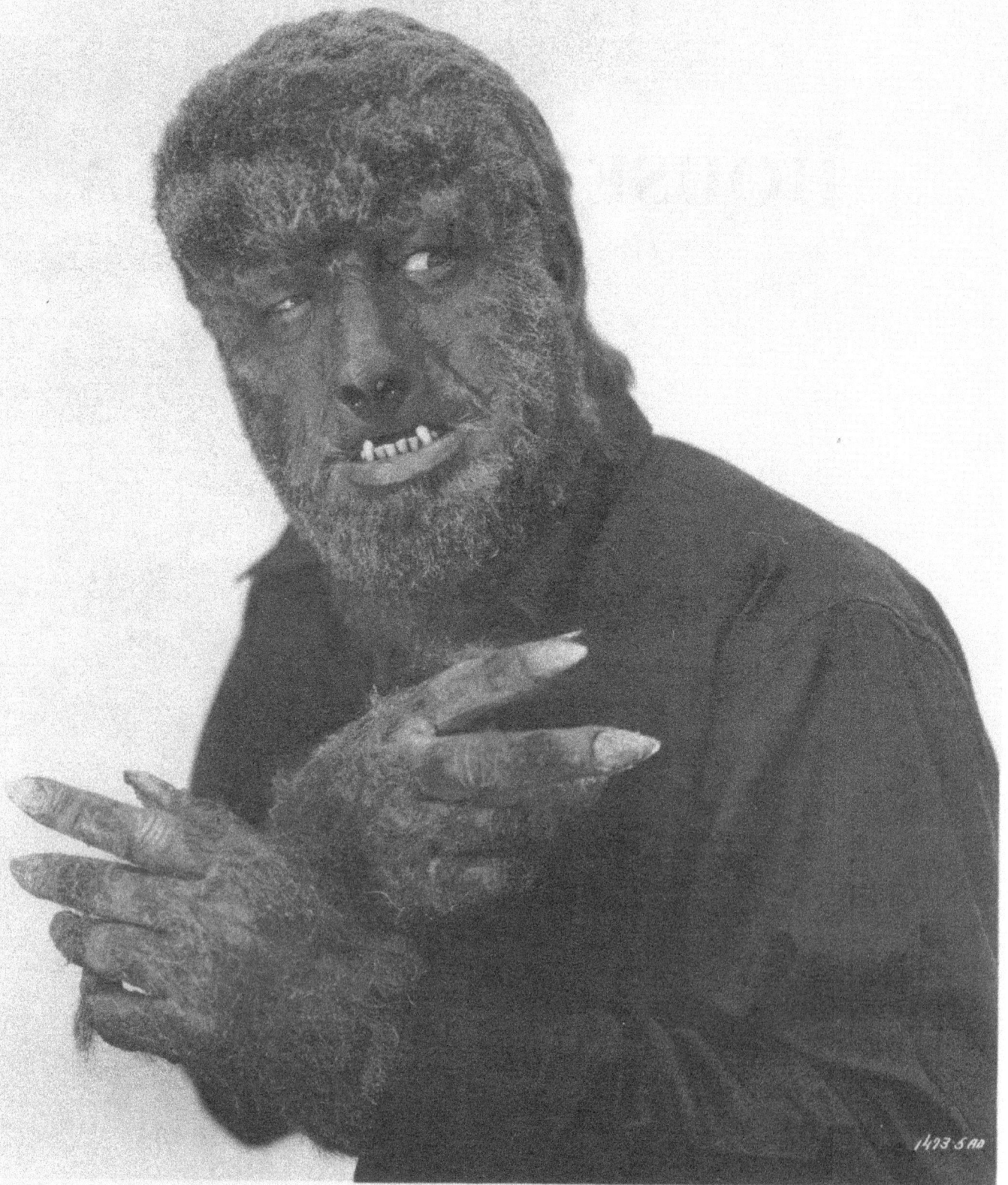

Lon Chaney in
"HOUSE OF DRACULA"
a Universal Production

45/378

HOUSE OF DRACULA

(The Original 1945 Shooting Script)

FIRST EDITION

Published by MagicImage Filmbooks, 740 S. 6th Avenue, Absecon, NJ 08201

Photographs, filmscript and other production materials used with the permission of and by special arrangement with Universal Studios.

The opinions expressed in this book are those of the individual authors and not the publisher.

The likeness of the late Lon Chaney Jr. used with permission of and by special arrangement between Hollywood Publishing Archives & Chaney Enterprises.

Contains the original shooting script by Edmund T. Lowe

The Library of Congress Cataloging-in Publication Data:

MagicImage Filmbooks presents House of Dracula : the original 1945
    shooting script / edited by Philip Riley ; interview with Jane Adams
    ; & production background by Gregory Wm. Mank ; foreword by Paul
Malvern ; introduction by John Carradine.
       p.   cm. -- (Universal filmscripts series. Classic horror
films ; v. 16)
    ISBN: 1-882127-19-6 : $19.95
    1. House of Dracula (Motion picture)   I. Riley, Philip J., 1948-
.   II. MagicImage Filmbooks (Firm) III. Title: House of Dracula.
IV. Series.
PN1997.H71125 1993
791.43'72--dc20   93-20464
                                  CIP

This edition published in the USA by:
BearManor Media • 1317 Edgewater Drive #110 • Orlando, Florida 32804
www.bearmanormedia.com

Hardcover: ISBN 978-1-62933-617-6
Paperback: ISBN 978-1-62933-616-9

The purpose of this series is the preservation of the art of writing for the screen. Rare books have long been a source of enjoyment and an investment for the serious collector, and even in limited printings there usually were a few thousand produced. Scripts however, numbered only 50 at the most, and we are proud to present them in their original form. Some will be final shooting scripts and some earlier drafts, so that students, libraries, archives and film-lovers might, for the first time, study them in their original form. In producing these volumes, we hope that the unique art of screenplay writing will be preserved for future generations.

1473-68A0

MAGICIMAGE PRODUCTIONS

Series Editor, Philip Riley

Art Director, Marisa Donato

Creative Consultant, Andrew Lee, Head of Research, Universal Studios, (retired)

Editorial Assistant - Christopher Mock

Cover Poster -Courtesy Cinema Collectors, Hollywood

Special Thanks to Bud Barnett
Cinema Collectors
1507 Wilcox Ave.
Hollywood, California 90028

The editor wishes to thank the following individuals and institutions for their generous assistance:

Ronald V. Borst
Caroline Carradine
Christopher Carradine
David Carradine
Ned Comstock
Nancy Cushing-Jones
Mathew Donato
Rita Duenas
Sue Dwiggins
Donald Fowle
Judd Funk
Ernest Goodman
Maria Jochsberger
Michelle Katz

Urbano Lemus
Linda Mehr
Doug Norwine
Gary Pasternack
Armondo Ponce
John Poorman
Ralph Renko
Anne Schlosser
Michael Sington
George Turner
Michael Voss
Wallace Worsley
Ralph Wrinkle

THE BILLY ROSE THEATER COLLECTION
    New York Public Library, Lincoln Center
The MARGARET HERRICK LIBRARY
    Academy of Motion Picture Arts and Sciences.
USC PERFORMING ARTS ARCHIVES
    Special Collections

Manufactured in the United States of America

Printed and bound by
McNaughton & Gunn Lithographers

Typesetting by Computer House, Absecon, New Jersey

The editor gratefully acknowledges the assistance and contributions provided by the following individuals in the preparation of this series over the past 25 years:

Jane Adams
Bud Abbott
Forrest J Ackerman
William Alland
Lew Ayres
William Bakewell
Ralph Bellamy
Stanley Bergerman
Robert Bloch
Richard Bojarski
Lincoln Bond
Ronald Borst
David Bradley
Ricou Browning
Kevin Brownlow
David Bruce
Ivan Butler
James Cagney
John Carradine
Ben & Ann Carre
Jeffery Carrier
Ronald Chaney
Lon Chaney Jr.
Ben Chapman
Virginia Christine
Carlos Clarens
Mae Clarke
Peter Coe
Franklin Coen
Ned Comstock
Mary Corliss
Bing Crosby
James Curtis
Nancy Cushing-Jones
Robert Cushman
Walter Daugherty
Gary Dorst
Harry Essex
Todd Feiertag
Bramwell Fletcher
Robert Florey
A. Arnold Gillespie
Ernest B. Goodman
Curtis Harrington
Tippi Hedren
Patricia Hitchcock
Valerie Hobson
Gloria Holden
Bob Hope
David S. Horsley
Henry Hull
Paul Ivano
Steven Jochsberger
Zita Johann
Raymond F. Jones
Boris Karloff
Michelle Katz
John Kobal

Jack Kevan
Poncho Kohner
Carl Laemmle Jr.
Carla Laemmle
Dorothy Lamour
Elsa Lanchester
John Landis
Janet Leigh
Celia Lovsky
Arthur Lubin
Paul Malvern
Raymond Massey
Rouben Mamoulian
Paul Mandell
Howard Mandlebaum
Gregory Wm. Mank
David Manners
Mike Mazurki
Lester Matthews
John McLaughlin
Scott McQueen
Lewis Milestone
Patsy Ruth Miller
Jeff Morrow
Douglas Norwine
Gary Pasternack
James Pepper
Anthony Perkins
Mary Philbin
Armando Ponce
Vincent Price
Claude Rains
Dr. Donald Reed
William Rosar
Margaret Ross
Hans J. Salter
Anne Schlosser
Martin Scorsese
Sherry Seeling
Wes Shank
David Skal
Curt Siodmak
Robert Skotak
Joseph Stefano
James Stewart
Glenn Strange
Kenneth Strickfaden
Gloria Stuart
Lupita Tovar
George Turner
Edward Van Sloan
Elena Verdugo
Maria Von Stroheim
Marc Wannamaker
Frank Westmore
Dan Woodruff
Wallace Worsley Jr.

JOHN CARRADINE

1906-1988

Good Night, Sweet Prince,

And Flights Of Angels

Sing Thee To Thy Rest

"Hollywood Reporter" December 6, 1988

Dedicated to
John Carradine

Something has spoken to me in the night,
burning the tapers of the waning years;
something has spoken in the night
and told me I shall die,
I know not where.
Saying:
To lose the earth you know,
for greater knowing;
to lose the life you have,
for greater life;
to leave the friends you loved,
for greater loving;
to find a land more kind than home
more large than earth - -
whereon the pillars of this earth
are founded,
toward which the conscience of the world
is tending - -
a wind is rising
and the rivers flow.

Thomas Wolfe

Foreword
by
Paul Malvern
Producer - *House of Dracula*

Paul Malvern in a production meeting with Glenn Cook, Assistant Production Manager at the Monogram Studios
(Courtesy Bison Archives)

I started out my career at Universal as a stunt man. Maybe that was the reason that we did so well with my War films and Westerns. I was a stunt man on the original 1925 *Phantom of the Opera* and met Chaney Sr. quite a few times on the lot. I did a fight scene, like an old bar room brawl from a Western, but it was cut out of the picture. It has been so long that I probably wouldn't even recognize my stunts if I saw the picture again today. If you are wondering how one goes from a stuntman to a producer I will tell you.

In 1927 I took a job as stunt double for John Barrymore in *The Beloved Rogue*. It was the story of François Villon shot at United Artists when they were still on Santa Monica Boulevard.

Barrymore was to save someone from the Bastille, probably Marceline Day.

Well, I thought that would be easy enough so I marched over to the Paris street set where there are about 300 extras waiting around. I see the director, Alan Crosland and Joe August the cameraman and next to him is a giant catapult! Alan said to me, "Hop on - you'll end up there." He indicated a 100 foot square net about 60 feet away. "What makes you think that I'm going to land directly in that net!" I told him and he said something like, "Well, Paul, the technicians have it all figured out mathematically." I said, "Right Alan, I just got off *The Trail of '98*

ALL THE THRILLS OF WILKIE COLLINS' FAMOUS NOVEL BROUGHT TO THE SCREEN!

MONOGRAM PICTURES Presents

THE MOONSTONE

AN UNSEEN MENACE THAT STRUCK IN THE NIGHT

DAVID MANNERS
PHYLLIS BARRY
Gustav von SEYFFERTITZ

might have been Rupert Julian (for whom I did some stunts at Universal for the Phantom in 1925.) Anyway, I'm supposed to dive off the mast of a big schooner and land in the ocean. Sounds easy enough on the ground. But when you get to the top of the mast, about 40 feet up, what is a little swell or wave in the ocean, translates to quite a ride when you're on a slim pole 40 feet in the air. The camera started to roll and a group of waves decide to come in at that time and I'm flying back and forth like a cartoon character and it comes time for me to jump and I launch myself off, miscalculated the punch (rocking of the ship) and it comes back too fast. I landed flat out spread eagle on the deck and was spitting blood for about 3 weeks. And that is how you go from a stunt man to a producer. While I was waiting for my new teeth to arrive I said to myself, There must be other things in this business I can do besides kill myself. So I took a job as an assistant director and moved up to being a producer. Those pictures with John Wayne and Bob Steele made up for the earlier years and I ended up at Universal.

In the 40s, Universal went through a big change. The cross-over years between the Laemmle's and the Cochrine/Cowers power structure of the late 30s were shaky. The Studio heads were Cliff Work and Nat Blumberg and I was one of their producers. The structure that we set up back then was the forerunner of the modern day television production company.

for Metro and we lost 6 men who tried stunts that were mathematically figured out! You're playing with my life here. Why don't you use a dummy! I won't be moving around if you shoot me out of that thing anyway. Unless you want me to flap my arms like a buzzard!''

They kept trying to get me into that catapult so finally I said, ''Look, I weigh 165 pounds. Let's put a sack of sand on that thing and you can shoot it into the scene and we'll see what happens.'' Well, they did and it went for one block and hit the top of the stage at the other end of the studio. And I said, ''There goes your mathematics all to hell!'' Eventually I did the stunt. I didn't tell them that there was a big difference between dead weight and live weight, but I wasn't about to take any chances. I had them rig up about 200 feet of rope net, including a 75 foot net going straight up between two telephone poles. I climbed in after another test; they pulled the cord and I went straight up about a hundred feet into the air; and even with all that precaution I was stopped by the top of the net by only about 10 feet. Barrymore got a big kick out of it! That wasn't the clincher though. A little later on I was on the Monogram lot, it might have been *The Yankee Clipper*. The director

JOHN WAYNE

HE DARED DEATH IN THE OUTLAW'S LAIR!

A LONE STAR WESTERN

THE STAR PACKER

A PAUL MALVERN PRODUCTION.
Written and Directed by ROBERT N. BRADBURY

Universal did not have a chain of theaters like MGM and Fox, so the war years became boom years, because of the pace set by Martin Murphy and the concentration on stock talent.

There were many well known bankable actors who were now free-lance; so many package deals could be made for special projects without keeping lots of high salary stars on contract for long periods of time. When a group of talent produced hits they became an in-house production team; Abbott and Costello, the Deanna Durbin films, my favorite, the Western and War films and of course, the monster films. My best memories were of the John Wayne films. John had been a western star, but it was our Universal films that launched him into becoming a big box office star.

I know the first thing that you are wondering. Why didn't Bela Lugosi play Dracula in my two monster films? I'm sure that since the Laemmle's were gone (he had had a big fight with them over the 2nd Dracula picture made in the 30s) [*Dracula's Daughter, 1936*] he probably was working at a different studio. Like I said, lots of actors were now free lance and the Screen Actor's Guild had formed around 1937. Being a producer, there were always casting ideas submitted by the directors. If there was someone that I thought would be better in the part I would win out! Universal did have a lot of talent on short term contracts and we always liked to use them as much as we could. You

Peter Coe

Peter Coe 1993, still in demand as a character actor, speaks many languages and is an acting coach.

get an actor like Peter Coe, who was the male lead in House of Frankenstein and you could always count on him for a good professional job. He could do Maria Montez pictures, War pictures, anything. Could never get him to sing though.

Technicolor was big then. We had lots of talent on the lot so I used Maria Montez and Andy Devine; but we brought Jon Hall over with Sabu for pictures like *Ali Baba and the 40 Thieves.*

Keep in mind now that the pictures that you will be reading about in this book were made under War Time restrictions. There was even a certain amount that we were allowed to spend on sets. I think it was $5,000.00, so that we could save lumber and nails for the War effort. Universal had the old European village and the Phantom's Opera House and the Notre Dame cathedral, we had our own lake, western villages, just about anything you wanted. But we mostly used the existing sets and kept spending down to a minimum.

Just the name Frankenstein was known to be an instant box office winner. So with *House of Frankenstein* on the big hit list for the previous year it was a natural to follow it up with *House of Dracula*. Only it wasn't called that at first. It was called *Dracula meets the Wolf Man*. Bela Lugosi was getting up in years and he couldn't handle the Frankenstein Monster role too well, so they started looking for ideas for him a few years back. We found the original story and sent it over to the censors office and they screamed bloody hell. There was so much real violence going on that I guess they were sensitive about what went on the screen. Lon Chaney was the Wolf Man. But the picture was shelved. The picture might have remained shelved but you never really got rid of a good story line.

After all the dust had settled over the final script and we knew who was going to play which monster, we were still missing the Frankenstein monster. Lon was the Wolf Man, Lugosi was making pictures over at Monogram and Karloff wouldn't have played the monster again if it meant a million dollars. I remembered Glenn Strange from the Westerns and sent him over to Erle, who sent him to Pierce and we had our man. Glenn played the monster in the last three Frankenstein films. He was a hell of a nice guy.

Curt Siodmak came up with the idea for the *House of Frankenstein* and we pulled out the old script for *Dracula Meets the Wolf Man* again and whipped it into shape for fast production as *House of Dracula.*

Lon Chaney Jr. was under contract and as far as the public was concerned, there were no other actors who could be the Wolf Man. He was a lot different than his father.

I was a very close friend of Lon Jr. There never was a nicer guy. He got along with everybody. He and Broderick Crawford and Andy Devine were all pals and they used to get together and do a lot of drinking. When we went on location [for *North of the Klondike*] to Big Bear (Califor-

The ending of House of Frankenstein as Glenn Strange (Frankenstein's Monster) carries Dr.Neimann (Boris Karloff) into the swamp

nia) the three of them didn't have to worry about keeping warm. If they weren't beating the hell out of each other, they drank enough to generate enough heat to keep us all warm!

I can't recall much about the technicians on the film. Being the producer, I always found it best to hire the finest crews and let them do their job. Unless the film started to go over budget. Jack Pierce had been around forever. He did all the makeup. John Fulton was the same. He was the best in the business when it came to in-camera effects.

At the end of the first "House" picture we had Glenn Strange carrying Boris Karloff into the swamp and they sink in the quicksand. I can remember that one. We set up a platform with a lift on it. The platform was set up in the tank and the crew took ground up cork and mixed it with the water. It made it look like mud. If we'd used real mud the actors would have suffocated. Once Glenn was in place we released the hydraulics on the lift and it looked like they were sinking in quick sand. Karloff was a real trouper for that one. He was not a young man at the time and I'm sure it wasn't a pleasant experience. Glenn was used to stuff like that. He had done quite a bit of stunt work and usually played the heavy in my westerns.

Erle Kenton and I got along beautifully. He was one director who thought everything out and made sure that he came in on budget and on time. He wasn't real fond of directing the Abbott and Costello films so he got a kick out of the monster films. He died about 13 years ago, from Parkinson's disease. Toward the end he didn't even know who I was when I would visit him. He married a woman named Claire, who was a wardrobe woman at Universal. I think they might have even met when we were making *North to the Klondike*.

Both of these films were enjoyable to make, the casts were all very nice to work with. They went on and did their business and that's all you can expect from them. The only problems that we had were the technical things. The electrical equipment would act up sometimes and throw off a scene. But these are problems that a producer must deal with.

I really didn't make many pictures that are in the category of this series of books. A few mysteries maybe; *The Mad Doctor of Market Street* with Lionel Atwill, *The Mystery of Marie Roget*, *The Moonstone*, but mostly I enjoyed the action packed westerns. I'm glad to be remembered for these two monster films. A producer is involved in the business end of movie making and often doesn't see the publicity or fame that an actor does. But even today, all you have to do is put either Dracula or Frankenstein in the title of a film and you are already part of history.

Paul Malvern
North Hollywood, 1991

The following list of Mr. Malvern's film credits was provided by the Academy of Motion Picture Arts and Science, Margaret Herrick Library. Most of the earlier films were done for Monogram. The first Universal credit was *Idol of the Crowds* which starred John Wayne. Even John Wayne acknowledged that it was through the support of Mr. Malvern that he rose from being an actor to a major star. [Additions and/or Corrections are welcome to preserve an accurate history]

Mr. Malvern can be seen on the critically acclaimed BBC Thirteen part 1980 Television Series "Hollywood" produced by Kevin Brownlow and David Gill, in "The Stuntman" segment. Available on Home Video.

1933 - *Breed of the Border, Trashing Broadway, Riders of Destry*

1934-5 - *Blue Steel, House of Mystery, Man from Utah, Monte Carlo Nights, The Moonstone, Mystery Trail, Arizona, Randy Rides Alone, Sage Brush, 16 Fathoms Deep, Trail Beyond, West of the Divide, Dawn Rider, Desert Trail, Lawless Frontier, Lawless West, New Frontier, Paradise Canyon, Rainbow Valley*

1936 - *King of the Pecos, The Lawless 90s, Oregon Trail Westward Ho!*

1937 - *Courage of the West, Idol of the Crowds, Singing Outlaw, Border Wolves*

1938 - *Prairie Justice, Western Trails, Air Devils*

1939 - *The Wolf Call, Danger Flight, The Phantom Stage, Mystery Plane, The Sky Patrol, The Stunt Pilot, Flying Cadets*
1940 - *Doomed to Die, Drums of the Desert, Phantom of China Town, Queen of the Yukon*

1941 - *Sign of the Wolf, Frisco Lil, Great Impersonator*
1942 - *North to the Klondike, The Mystery of Marie Roget, Halfway to Shanghai, The Mad Doctor of Market Street, The Mystery Gambler*

1943 - *A Cowboy in Manhattan, Follow the Band, Good Morning Judge, Hi Buddy!*

1944 - *Ali Baba and the 40 Thieves, House of Frankenstein*
1945 - *House of Dracula, Sudan*

1946 - *Tangiers, Pirates of Monterey*

1950 - *Rock Island Trail*

Boris Karloff, Director Erle C. Kenton, Elena Verdugo and Producer Paul Malvern on the set of
House of Frankenstein

To Phil —
Best wishes
John Carradine

Introduction
by
John Carradine

John Carradine applies his makeup for the character of Dracula in this publicity photograph. The actual makeup was applied by the makeup crew headed by Jack Pierce.

Monsters, monsters, monsters! What macabre fascination does this character, Dracula, hold on the minds of our culturally impotent society? I speak mainly of the Western Coast and a great portion of the Eastern Coast with the exception of portions of New York and the City of New Orleans in the South.

DRACULA - The role holds a curse greater than Hamlet! Give the audience Richard III, Othello, The Merchant of Venice and what will they remember? A Vampyer! Do the youth of today remember Reverend Casy of *The Grapes of Wrath*? (Try rolling your Rs on that one while sober.) One would think that, for these modern couples, the experience of having children would satisfy anyone's curiosity for monsters.

I pity anyone who plays the part. Universal remade the film again. I suppose someday a true adaptation of Stoker's novel will be made. To date, I have the distinction of being the only actor who looked the part as visualized by Bram Stoker in 1897. Dracula was a Magyar. When he first appears to Jonathan Harker he is an old man with long white hair and a moustache. It would have been impossible to speak lines with a mouth full of sharp teeth, so I settled on the long hair and white moustache. The studio refused to allow me to keep the long hair, but the moustache remained. For some reason they needed to make the character in the mold of the Wolf Man for the second film [*House of Frankenstein*, 1944 and *House of Dracula*, 1945]. I played the character as evil as possible for I

John Carradine as Dracula in 1977 on TV's "McCloud"

learned long ago that if I wanted to continue to eat, villains find steadier work than artists. The public will remember a villain. The story writer [Curt Siodmak] of the first film at least had talent and credibility. He knew what he was writing about for he came from the area where the legends were told around gypsy campfires. However the scriptwriter knew as much about the characters as his paycheck would allow! They ended up making Dracula a type of dope fiend. Instead of existing as the traditional vampire, he now was seeking out the help of a doctor to cure him of his vampirism by the use of modern medical means. But instead the doctor's blood gets contaminated by the vampires and he becomes evil.

If made today I could understand the public's interest in such a character. One who is addicted to drugs, like many of today's youth, is the vampire. He knows that he is doing something wrong, and yet he cannot stop himself. In Stoker's day it was more sexual repression than drugs. Drugs were popular and readily available in drink and powders. Absinthe being one drink considered a social drink, and yet it was very addicting. The vampire must drink blood from his victim every night to sustain his existence. He cannot enter a house or a bedroom unless invited. Once his victim is bitten she becomes an addict who craves for the nightly visits, gives up normal drinking and eating habits. Eventually the obsession causes death and although of no use to the vampire, the victim then becomes a vampire herself. This would be another form of public identity. The dope pusher gives his victim a sample of his drugs. Soon the victim is dependent on him and his or her body is dependent on the drugs. Soon all that has been good in life is sacrificed for the sake of the obsession and sometimes the person dies. Blood has always been a symbol of life. The drug or drink is carried in the blood. Diseases are carried in the blood. Back in the 40s one of President Roosevelt's sons died from blood poisoning caused by the dye of a sock getting into a cut on his foot. The fear of this caused the sales of white socks to sky-rocket. But if you wanted to show that you were tough and not afraid, a symbol of power among the youth was the wearing of black or colored socks. In the repressed Victorian era Stoker gave us one of the most erotic examples of Gothic literature. The thrill of a secret lover. The excitement of doing something bad, of giving into the power of the flesh, these were the day dreams of the young and the nightmares of the parents.

I suppose that is the curse of Dracula for any actor who portrays the character. The public identifies in Dracula a release from the restraints of society. What young maiden could resist a story about a tall, dark stranger who would come into their lives and take them away from their square families or their corporate trainee fiancé whose only ambition in life is to have the biggest car on the block or own a color television set? This horror was a worse fate than losing one's soul.

But the actor is so closely linked to the identity of Dracula, that any attempt to break that identity and the public treats you like a mistress who insists that you leave your wife and family and forces a confrontation.

By the time they were finished the script, millions of GI's were being shipped home. World War II had ended. Many of those GI's did not come home whole in mind and body. Thousands of families had their own horrors at home to contend with and the studios were running scared from any type of horror film. The public now wanted musicals and light fantasy. The horror and monster company on the lot was reduced to what could be compared today as a weekly television soap opera or series. They even gave the great makeup artist Jack Pierce the boot after this film. I could see that coming along much earlier. Jack was a genius. The monster game was all the idea of young Laemmle, the son of the founder of Universal. [Carl Laemmle Sr. 1867-1939]

He [Laemmle Jr.] knew what he wanted on screen and if a person had the right talent to make it happen for him, they had a job and all the tools they needed to do that job. The boy, whose real name was Julius, loved Lon Chaney Sr.'s films. When he was given control of the studio at the age of 21 he took his father's name. I think the monster films were his way of getting back at his father for the control that was put on him.

Jack Pierce, the makeup man, could give him his

monsters. Pierce was a feisty little guy who took great pride in his work. He only had one assistant. He not only did monsters; he could turn aging fat actresses into beauties and the necessary young handsome leading man into any age called for by the script. He did all the work himself, not like those who followed and had a crew of lackeys to do all the work while they played golf and took all the credit. Pierce enjoyed the protection of young Laemmle and when the old man lost the studio the new managers did not know how to handle him. He didn't take any crap from anyone and expected his long standing title of "Director of Makeup" to carry him through any dispute, be it an actress or director. That is what got him canned. The new group, once they found out that others could copy his work, cheaper, just waited for him to show his usual spunk and used that as an excuse to fire him.

But by the forties, it [Universal] was like a factory anyway and there was little room for creative talent when it stood in the way of box office profits. The studio had little interest in making big budget pictures. It actually was very much the counterpoint of the television industry today.

My recollections of the making of these two films, in which I portrayed the Count, are few. I had taken on the parts to finance my own company. I did not see much of Lon Chaney on the set. We did however, meet at the local watering hole after hours with his other drinking buddies, Broderick Crawford and Andy Devine. Of Glenn Strange, I recall nothing. That is not to say that our paths did not cross from time to time in recent television films and in some of the westerns that were being made simultaneously on the same backlot. Martha Driscoll and Jane Adams were stock players, both very pretty and pleasant. Producer Malvern seemed more at home with his western classics. I believe that he was the one who gave John Wayne's career a boost and made him a star.

Universal is a strange place. It seems to have a life of its own no matter who owns it! Since this is all that you are going to get out of me about the monster films, I might as well tell you that I got my start at Universal in *The Invisible Man* (1933). I had seen the Invisible Man riding a bicycle and ran to a phone booth to report it to Scotland Yard. A few years later I was given another small part by James Whale in *The Bride of Frankenstein* (1935) as a hunter who stumbles upon Boris Karloff in the old Hermit's hut. Whale was a strange chap. His career existed solely because of Laemmle Jr. *The Bride of Frankenstein* was one of the last pictures for the original owners of Universal. There were undercurrents that the studio would be sold every week, but it wasn't until a year later that it finally happened. Even then everything that was produced in this field [monster films] was a result of the Laemmle years. Stories purchased in the 30s were rehashed or brought out of the vaults and reworked. I have always been amazed how Universal always gives birth to a genre and then

allows them to get away in the remake game. The British remade the old titles in the 50s and made a fortune. RKO remade *The Hunchback of Notre Dame*. Disney has their cartoons, MGM had their musicals, but Universal is known for their monsters. Let us hope that this series of books by Phil Riley for MagicImage has some influence. All that it really takes is for someone to care - and for someone with the cash in hand to listen! Take it from me, one with great experience on the subject of Universal Pictures. You new owners do not just own the ground where your new Tours are flourishing - you also own the mineral rights and there is a gold mine right under your feet.

But my advice to Mr. Riley, in his passionate plea for the preservation of the old Universal monsters from the European legends is; in his ancestral Celtic tongue:

Nid yw prophwyd heb anrhydedd, ond yn ei wlad ei hun, ac yn ei dy ei hun. Matthew 13:57

Now kiddies' as my grandfather, the founder of the Methodist Holy Rollers sect would say, "Risk ye not the fires of Hell! Out then with the Good Book and learn ye well."

John Carradine
San Diego, Ca. 1986

Editor's note: This introduction was planned well in advance of the production of this series by MagicImage Filmbooks. It was pieced together from many visits with Mr. Carradine, both at his various homes and in accompanying him on his Concert readings around southern California. He had approved the text that you have just read in 1986. We had made plans to finish the final copy and fill in the gaps upon his return from Africa where he was filming his last picture in 1988.

After discovering that his plane was to have a long layover in Milan Italy, he decided to visit the ancient cathedral, Il Duomo di Milano (known for its mountain of stairs, often used by pilgrims to do penance by climbing them on their knees or even face down). Upon finding that the elevator was out of order he was determined it would be worth the effort to view the sculpture and beauty of the cathedral. At age 82 he attempted to climb the steps. It was too much for his heart. John Carradine passed away on November 27, 1988.

For a complete listing of Mr. Carradine's films and more about his life read, "The Hollywood Hissables" by Gregory Wm. Mank published by Scarecrow, NJ 1989.

Jane Adams in her role as the hunchback nurse, Nina

An Interview with
Jane Adams
by
Gregory Wm. Mank

Nicknamed "Poni" because of her riding abilities, Jane Adams receives her own folding chair, a status symbol in the studio system.

In Universal's Horror Mythology, pathos was always a dynamic, often profound characteristic. Most of the studio's goblins possessed it in magical abundance, such as Karloff's Frankenstein Monster, with his scarred, pleading, heartbreaking hands, and Chaney's Wolf Man, with his agonized glances at the full moon. It even lurked behind Claude Rains' most megalomaniacal cackles in *The Invisible Man*, Bela Lugosi's austere, regal loneliness in *Dracula*, and Karloff's lovesick mysticism in *The Mummy*.

In the final serious entry of Universal's Frankenstein saga, 1945's *House of Dracula*, the studio introduced a new horror character: Nina, the hunchbacked nurse to miracle-working Dr. Franz Edelmann. Universal required an actress who was not only beautiful (to add to the irony of her deformity), but sufficiently gifted to play the part with drama, and delicacy.

Fortunately, at the time, Universal had Jane Adams on contract.

A former Conover model, with a fine background in the Arts, Miss Adams created a haunting appeal and pathos as Nina, the melodrama tossing her near the clutches of Chaney's Wolf Man, Carradine's Count Dracula, Glenn Strange's Frankenstein Monster, and (fatally) Onslow Stevens' Jekyll/Hyde, Dr. Edelmann. Her sensitive portrayal added a depth to this Monster Rally, and her death scene - strangled by the mad Edelmann, whom she admired and loved so much - gave the movie a true touch of tragedy.

Long considered a lost player by film historians, Miss Adams retired from acting 40 years ago. She has been married to the same gentleman for over 45 years, has two children and four grandchildren. Recently she graciously spoke with me about her days at Universal, and the filming of House of Dracula, from her home in the posh desert community of Rancho Mirage, under the mountains near Palm Springs, California.

Could you please give us some information about your early background?

I was born in San Antonio, Texas, but we moved to California when I was 2. When I was 4 years old, (this probably sounds boastful, but I don't mean it to!) I was tested, and found to have the second highest I.Q. in the State of California. And then I went on and became a concert mistress of the Los Angeles all-city high school orchestra. All of which is to say that I had a background in the Arts - and the big thing for me was attending the Pasadena Playhouse.

The Pasadena Playhouse is legendary in the talent who trained there.

Oh, it was great! We had three stages - main stage, lab stage, and theatre-in-the-round. We started in that school with Roman tragedies and went all the way up through Modern drama. We did everything, read everything, had classes all day in fencing, costume design, history of the theatre - everything. So I had my Theatre Arts degree from there.

What led to the Universal contract?

I was a Conover model, working in New York City. I had made 4 or 5 covers, and a full-page picture for ESQUIRE magazine. Walter Wanger, the producer, saw it and asked me to come out to Hollywood for a screen test. The film was Universal's *Salome Where She Danced* (1945), and Yvonne de Carlo got the part, but I did get a nice contract. They had signed about five girls at that time, but they soon let all of them go except Yvonne and me.

Jane Adams and Glenn Strange on the set of House of Dracula

I really think the thing that enabled me to stay there was my 4 years at the Pasadena Playhouse; they knew that, thanks to my training, they could give me any script.

Did you enjoy moving from stage work and modeling to Universal movies?

I LOVED it. I found everybody very congenial. It was an interesting time for me. I married my husband on Bastille Day, July 14, 1945 - and two days later, he was sent overseas for 14 months. So it was good to be busy working until he came back.

What led directly to being cast as Nina in House of Dracula?

Really, I think it was my size! I'm only 5' 3", and I think that's one reason I got into horror films, because I'm not the chorus girl type; rather short compared to the other girls who were under contract.

Did you have any resentment, after being a Conover model, at being cast as a hunchback?

No, I LOVED to do character parts. I never thought of myself as a glamour girl - I wanted serious parts. Are you familiar with "Gods of the Lightning," one of Maxwell Anderson's plays? It was about the Sacco/Vanzetti case, one of the big law cases of the 1920s; they had a whole room of research on it at the Los Angeles public library. It was a very heavy dramatic part, and I had done it at the Playhouse. So I loved that sort of thing.

What was the atmosphere like on the set of House of Dracula?

Well, I was familiar with Onslow Stevens and John Carradine, who acted on the stage at Pasadena Playhouse...really fine actors. On *House of Dracula*, my memory is that they were ALL very serious actors, and they were sitting around, studying their scripts. The makeup was uncomfortable (for them, particularly), and my cast weighed a lot; it was made of Plaster of Paris, before they used plastics. It was all quite a serious thing - the script was heavy and serious.

There's a famous candid shot of you posing and laughing with Glenn Strange as Frankenstein's Monster.

Oh yes! He was a VERY nice man. EVERYBODY was on that set. Martha O'Driscoll was very nice, very helpful to me, because I didn't really know anything about movie-making, having trained in stage technique at the Playhouse.

So, all in all, I just had a very rich experience. It was a great set, and a great studio.

You went on to do all kinds of things at Universal: the serial Lost City of The Jungle, westerns...

Yes, because I knew how to ride.

One of your best-remembered roles was the blind pianist of The Brute Man, with Rondo Hatton, the acromegliac actor then on contract to Universal.

Yes. That was both an interesting and challenging experience. The progressive state of Rondo's disease made it very difficult for him to remember his script and always be responsive - but, overall, he did a good job. It's unfortunate that he died soon after we made *The Brute Man* (1946)

After leaving Universal, you did films at Monogram, TV episodes of "The Cisco Kid" with Duncan Renaldo and Leo Carrillo, "Dangerous Assignment" TV episode with Brian Donlevy...

Eventually I settled down with my husband (who retired from the Military as a Major General) and our family. Now I'm living in Palm Springs, right on a golf course, and it's beautiful - the most gorgeous view in the world of the mountains!

Since your years at Universal City, have you ever returned there, for the tour?

No - but I'd love to go!

[A partial credit list of Jane Adams]

- *House of Dracula* 1945; *The Lost City of the Jungle, A Night in Paradise, The Brute Man* 1946; *Master Minds, Batman and Robin* (Vicki Vale) 1949; "The Ghost Wolf" SUPERMAN television Episode, 1955

Onslow Stevens turned evil after his blood was tainted by Dracula's blood during a transfusion.

HOUSE OF DRACULA
Production Background
by
Gregory Wm. Mank

The main entrance to Universal Studios in the mid-40s - now the site of the Executive offices or "The Black Tower"

**The Screen's MIGHTIEST Monsters Thrash Out
AGAINST the Frenzy OF THE MOB!**
- from Universal's HOUSE OF DRACULA trailer

In 1945, the crazy, carnival world of cowboys and saloon girls, harem sirens and horses, glamour girl sopranos, roustabout comics and beloved Monsters that was Universal City in the War Years hit a wild, prolific climax. The FILM DAILY YEARBOOK tallied Universal's 1945 product at (appropriately) 45 feature films - some sparked by the lot's most popular and legendary attractions.

Deanna Durbin sang Danny Boy in *Because of Him*, and played an oomphy femme fatale in the mystery thriller, *Lady on The Train*.

Abbott and Costello cavorted in *Here Come the Co-Eds (*in which Lou posed as a female basketball player) and *The Naughty Nineties* (with Bud and Lou reprising their classic Who's on First?).

Maria Montez slinked through the lush Technicolor of *Sudan* flanked by Jon Hall, and menaced by a wonderfully wicked George Zucco.

Basil Rathbone and Nigel Bruce teamed again in three SHERLOCK HOLMES melodramas: *The House of Fear*, *The Woman in Green* (in which they foiled Henry Daniell's Moriarty) and *Pursuit to Algiers*.

Gloria Jean trilled in *Easy To Look At* and *I'll Remember April*; Olsen and Johnson clowned in *See My Lawyer*; Donald O'Connor and Peggy Ryan cut a rug in *Patrick The Great*; the Andrews Sisters jived in *Her Lonely Night;*

Alan Curtis, Kent Taylor and Lon Chaney galloped in *The Daltons Ride Again*; and Susanna Foster (of 1943's *Phantom of the Opera)*, in chorus girl frills and tights, revealed her figure in *Frisco Sal* ("It was well worth waiting for," hailed THE HOLLYWOOD REPORTER).

There were four super serials: *Jungle Queen, The Master Key, Secret Agent X-9* and *The Royal Mounted Ride Again*; five Woody Woodpecker one-reelers; nine Name Band one-reel musicals; two one-reel Swing Symphonies...

And, of course, there were Universal's horror shows. The Lon Chaney Inner Sanctums included *The Frozen Ghost* (featuring the Universal swan song of a pregnant Evelyn Ankers), *Strange Confession* (an updating of the 1934 Claude Rains vehicle *The Man Who Reclaimed His Head*, with Chaney, Brenda Joyce and J. Carrol Naish respectively inheriting the Rains, Joan Bennett and Lionel Atwill roles) and *Pillow of Death*. *The Mummy's Curse*, the 5th Mummy saga, brought Chaney Jr. back as Kharis, with Virginia Christine as his resurrected ancient love; *Jungle Captive* found Vicky Lane replacing Acquanetta as Paula the Ape Woman in the saga inaugurated by *Captive Wild Woman* (1943) and perpetuated in *Jungle Woman* (1944).

However, Universal's Big Horror Show of the year had been *House of Frankenstein*, nationally released February 16, 1945 (following New York and Hollywood premieres in December of 1944). Mad Doctor Karloff (with an assist from homicidal hunchback J. Carrol Naish) had resurrected Chaney's Wolf Man, John Carradine's Count Dracula, and Glenn Strange's Frankenstein Monster - all to super box office.

And now, come the Fall of 1945, Universal couldn't resist yet another Monster Rally to show off its powerhouse goblins.

****

Universal's Super-Sequel to Record-Wrecking HOUSE OF FRANKENSTEIN...The Same BIG Sell...Geared to Even BIGGER Grosses!
- Universal Trade Publicity for HOUSE OF DRACULA

In December of 1944, as Universal was preparing the premiere of *House of Dracula*, the studio prepared a new horror brainchild: Wolf Man Vs. Dracula. On December 4, 1944, Joseph Breen, Hollywood's almighty censor, dictated this letter to Universal after perusing the script:

...It is imperative that you exercise the greatest restraint at all times in avoiding excessive gruesomeness and horror angles, not only to comply with the provisions of the Production Code relating to these points, but further to avoid considerable deletions by political censor boards...

...you must omit the sounds of the stake being driven into the body and the ear-splitting scream...

...In scene 21, we request that your rephrase the first sentence to read, "He was APPARENTLY dead," inserting the underscored word...to avoid offense to persons of sincere religious convictions...

...In scene 76 there should be no unacceptable exposure of Yvonne's person, and we request further that she put on some sort of a bathrobe at this point...

...In scene 284, instead of having the words "Oh God come through," we request this be changed to something else, possibly "Merciful Heaven..."

Universal had lined up production for "Wolf Man vs. Dracula," with Ford Beebe set to direct. Long with Universal, Beebe had slickly directed the Lugosi serial *The Phantom Creeps* (1939) and the Lugosi/Atwill feature *Night Monster* (1942), produced *Son of Dracula* (1943), and produced AND directed *The Invisible Man's Revenge* (1944). However, following Mr. Breen's letter, production of "Wolf Man Vs. Dracula" fell through. Posterity would never know if Yvonne put on her bathrobe!

Come February of 1945, however, a variation loomed on Universal's production blueprints: *House of Dracula*.

In late Summer of 1945, amidst the euphoria of a World War II victory, Universal officially launched this new Monster rally, to unite the Wolf Man, Dracula, the Frankenstein Monster, a Mad Doctor - and even a female hunchback. The shooting title: DESTINY. (This working title haunted the writing quarters of Universal City; it had been the original title of *The Wolf Man*, had passed on as the original script title of *House of Dracula*, and even remained so after Universal's 1944 Gloria Jean vehicle that WAS entitled DESTINY!).

Basically a sequel to *House of Frankenstein*, *House of Dracula* would reunite many of that 1944 production's alumni: Producer Paul Malvern (who, in the interim, had produced Maria Montez's *Sudan*); Executive Producer Joseph Gershenson; Director Erle C. Kenton. Even the script writer was the same: Edward T. Lowe (basing his screenplay on the uncredited story of George Bricker and Dwight Babcock). The script would make no attempt to explain the resurrection of Dracula and the Wolf Man - and, for a surprise, placed Visaria (village locale in The *Ghost of Frankenstein, Frankenstein Meets the Wolf Man* and *House of Frankenstein*) atop the cliffs of a seacoast.

The "gimmick:" all the legendary monsters wanted a cure, and visited miracle-working scientist Dr. Franz Edelmann, congregating at his seaside castle.

Top-billed Lon Chaney played the Wolf Man, his "baby," for the 4th time. Lon discovered that the shooting script not only afforded him a cure for his Lycanthropy - but also made him the hero of the melodrama, and gave

Lon Chaney Jr.

him the leading lady! (To assure that the Wolf Man could pass the censor muster as a hero, the script had to make sure Larry Talbot severed no jugulars this time out.) Chaney now was enjoying his 1300-acre retreat in El Dorado County, California, which he christened Lennie's Ranch (named, of course, after his heartbreaking character in Of Mice and Men). Between films, Lon worked the ranch, raising cattle, assisted by his own teenage sons, Lon and Ronald.

"If this goes over," John Carradine had vowed of his repertory stage company, JOHN CARRADINE AND HIS SHAKESPEARE PLAYERS, "I'm through with Hollywood forever!" Carradine's classical portrayals of Hamlet, Shylock, and Othello had won bravos, and the actor had glorious dreams of devoting himself to the Theatre with his new blonde bride, Sonia (who later became mother to Keith, Christopher and Robert Carradine). However, Carradine had made unhappy headlines that summer when his first wife (mother of Bruce and David Carradine) had her ex-spouse tossed in jail for "alimony contempt." Back from Coney Island, where he had starred with Sonia in a stock production of the farce "My Dear Children" (in the role played on Broadway by his idol, John Barrymore), Carradine honored Universal's offer to return to the cape and opera hat of Count Dracula.

John Carradine as Count Dracula

(Incidentally, Bela Lugosi, Universal's original Dracula, had just completed work as Lionel Atwill's butler in *Genius at Work,* an Alan Carney/Wally Brown RKO farce, not released until late 1946. While *Genius at Work* was finished in time for Bela to join *House of Dracula,* he apparently received no overture to reprise the Count, and Carradine was Universal's top choice for the Vampire King.)

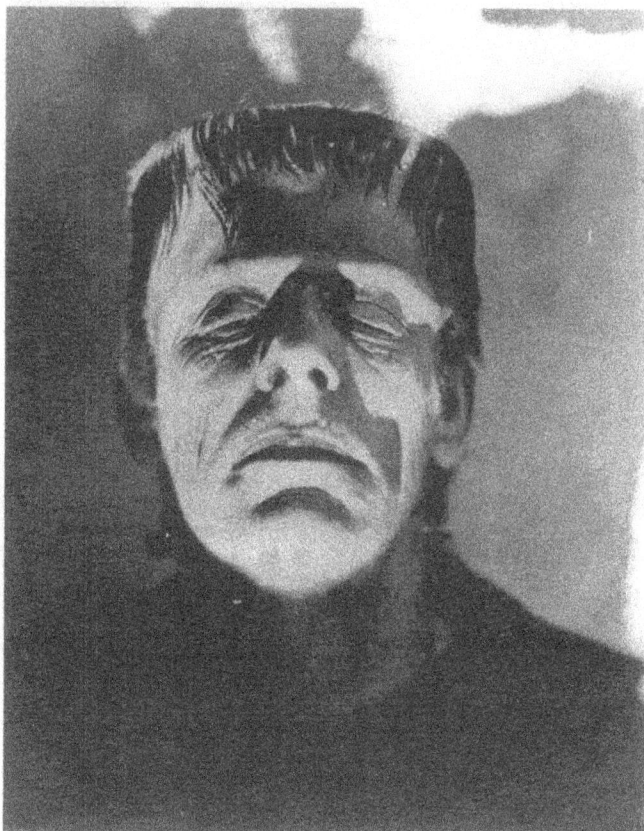

Martha O'Driscoll

However, the most striking female performance in *House of Dracula* would be Jane "Poni" Adams as Nina, the pathetic hunchbacked nurse.

Glenn Strange as Frankenstein's Monster

For Frankenstein's Monster, Universal once again signed Glenn Strange, who had played the creature in *House of Frankenstein.* Since the first Monster rally, the ex-Texas cowboy had returned to sagebrush in Universal's *Renegades of The Rio Grande* (1945), and was happy to meet again with Jack Pierce for his 3-hour transformations into Mary Shelley's immortal Monster.

For the leading female role of Miliza Morelle, nurse to Dr. Edelmann, Universal selected Martha O'Driscoll. The beautiful, blonde, Oklahoma-born actress had made her Universal bow in 1937's *She's Dangerous* (as The Blonde Girl), followed by a bit in Deanna Durbin's 1938 *Mad About Music* (as The Pretty Girl) before signing with Paramount. She became a Universal contract attraction in 1943. In the course of *House of Dracula,* Miss O'Driscoll would have to sacrifice a little feminine pride by affecting green makeup (which photographed a pallid white) for her famous seduction by Dracula, while playing Moonlight Sonata at piano.

Jane Adams as Nina, the Hunchback

The real staring role of House of Dracula, however, was Dr. Franz Edelmann - the brilliant scientist transformed into a Jekyll/Hyde beast by the blood of Dracula. The role is so rich, one might imagine that Universal had

Onslow Stevens

Skelton Knaggs - center

envisioned it for Karloff (who was then at RKO, happily starring in such Val Lewton chillers as *The Body Snatcher*, *Isle of the Dead* and *Bedlam*). However, the part went to character player Onslow Stevens. Born March 29, 1902 in Los Angeles, Stevens had an illustrious career on the stage of the Pasadena Playhouse, and was busy at Universal City in the early 1930s, playing in such films as *Once in a Lifetime* (1932), *The Secret of the Blue Room* (1933, with Lionel Atwill and Gloria Stuart), *Counsellor at Law* (1933, with John Barrymore), *Life Returns* (1935, based on Dr. Robert Cornish's restoration of life to a dead dog at USC in 1934) - as well as such serials as 1934's *The Vanishing Shadow*. Lacking the box office name of Chaney and Carradine, Stevens had to settle for only feature billing, even thought the Edelmann role totally dominated *House of Dracula*.

The supporting cast boasted Skelton Knaggs as Steinmuhl, the village creep who climactically leads the Visaria mob against Edelmann's castle. An English-born Shakespearean mime, Knaggs was marketing his pock-marked features and eerie tenor voice to various studios: to RKO's Val Lewton for The *Ghost Ship* (1943), *Isle of the Dead* (1945) and *Bedlam* (completed in midsummer of 1945, and released in 1946); to 20th Century-Fox for *The Lodger* (1944); to MGM for *The Picture of Dorian Grey* (1945). Knaggs had even played on Broadway in the melodrama "Hand in Glove" (1944) as "Hughie", a Chaney-like grotesque, and directed by none other than

James Whale (Universal's legendary Director of *Franken-stein*, *The Old Dark House*, *The Invisible Man* and *The Bride of Frankenstein*). Knaggs already had one Universal horror film in his credits (1944's *The Invisible Man's Revenge*) when he reported for *House of Dracula*.

Playing Steinmuhl's brother, Ziegfried (fated to have his throat torn out by the mad Edelmann) was Ludwig Stossel, plump German player, and veteran of such thrill-ers as MGM's *Hitler's Madman* (1943), Universal's *The Climax* and PRC's *Bluebeard* (both 1944). Stossel would go on to play Einstein in MGM's 1947 *The Beginning or the End* - and, decades later, became famous on television commercials as The Little Old Winemaker!

Finally, and most dramatically, Lionel Atwill - one-armed Inspector Krogh of *Son of Frankenstein*, mad Dr. Bohmer of *The Ghost of Frankenstein* the Mayor of *Frankenstein Meets the Wolf Man* and Inspector Arnz of *House of Frankenstein* - signed to play Inspector Holtz, making his 5th appearance in a Universal Frankenstein saga, and awarded 4th billing on the starring credits. Shortly after completing *House of Frankenstein*, Atwill had married his 4th wife, Paula Pruter, in Las Vegas on July 7, 1944. Now, as *House of Dracula* began shooting, the 60-year old actor and his 28-year old wife were only days away becoming parents. It all seemed a wonderful new life for Atwill, who had survived his ugly sex scandal of the early 1940s and was facing his tomorrows with Paula and their child-to-be.

Tragically, however, Atwill himself was fatally ill - with bronchial cancer. As Atwill reported for night shoot-ing on the old European Village set, parading authorita-tively as Inspector Holtz, nobody could have expected that the dynamic trouper had only 6 months to live.

Edward T. Lowe fine-tuned the script of House of Dracula working on re-writes right up to the eve of shooting. Jack P. Pierce once again prepared his makeup laboratory for the monsters, while George Robinson - cinematographer of *Son of Frankenstein*, *Frankenstein*

Lionel Atwill as Inspector Holtz

Meets the Wolfman, The Spanish *Dracula (1931) and House of Frankenstein* - prepared to capture the Gothic vision of what would be Universal's last serious adventure of Dracula, the Wolf Man and Frankenstein's Monster.

Late in the week of September 17, 1945, *House of Dracula* began shooting.

_____

**One Monster Would Be Terrific...
But Here Are
FIVE
To Bring You Five
Times the Thrill.....**

- from the trailer for HOUSE OF DRACULA.

_____

House of Dracula filmed smoothly and happily throughout the early Fall of 1945, as Universal City shared the joy of the nation with the World War finally over. It was a happy lot, and other Universal films in production simultaneously with *House of Dracula* were *Because of Him*, starring Deanna Durbin, Franchot Tone and Charles Laughton; the Maria Montez vehicle, *Tangier*, featuring Preston Foster, Sabu, and *Son of Dracula* alumni Robert Paige and Louise Albritton; The *Spider Woman Strikes Back*, with Gale Sondergaard and Rondo Hatton; and the super Susan Hayward/Dana Andrews/Brian Donlevy western, *Canyon Passage* (In which Onslow Stevens had a supporting role).

The ghoulish spectacle of *House of Dracula* proved a popular attraction on the Universal lot. Lon Chaney's sons, 17-year old Lon and 15-year old Ronald, paid a visit to the set - where young Lon delighted the publicity boys by jokingly pretending to strangle his infamous Dad. Veteran Universal contractee Andy Devine brought his young sons to the *House of Dracula* soundstage, where they sat on the lap of the Frankenstein Monster.

John Carradine and Martha O'Driscoll pose with Lon Chaney Jr. when his two sons Ronald (left) and Lon III (strangling Chaney) visit the set. Ronald Chaney died in 1990 and Lon Chaney III died in late 1992 in an automobile accident.

Tad and Dennis Devine, sons of comic character actor, Andy Devine visit the set of House of Dracula, *while they were filming* Canyon Passage *in another part of the studio. Studio press release has Dennis quoted as saying "Gee, you're as tall as my dad is round." Strange stood 7'2" in the monster outfit.*

Professionalism and camaraderie dominated the shooting - as well as the usual mischief. Many years later, Glenn Strange revealed in Donald F. Glut's book, *The Frankenstein Legend* (Scarecrow Press, 1973), how he survived the scene in which Edelmann and Talbot find the Monster in the cave quicksand, cradling the skeleton of *House of Frankenstein's* Dr. Niemann:

"Remember when I was lying in the quicksand in HOUSE OF DRACULA and the opening scene had me with the skeleton of Karloff? Well, I was in there all day long and that stuff was cold! They poured it down a chute and into this cave-like thing. And Chaney came down with a fifth and I think I got most of it. He poured it down me and it warmed me up some. They finished shooting and I went up to the dressing room. Of course they had a nice fire up there. They took the makeup off and by the time I got about half undressed I was so looped I could hardly get up. I got warm. And then I got tight. But I think he just about saved my life that day."

There also were some cost-cutting economy measures. Universal's old set from *Tower of London* (1939) represented Edelmann's Visaria castle (just as it had stood in for both Neustadt Prison and Niemann's castle in *House of Frankenstein*). Also, according to the *House of Dracula* pressbook, the yak hair that comprised Chaney's Wolf Man makeup had run dangerously low - Universal had not received a fresh shipment of yak hair (via Central Asia) since before the War. Jack Pierce discovered that, through judicious application, he had just enough yak hair left to glue onto Chaney for his two brief appearances as the Wolf Man. (It was just as well; since Chaney was the hero this time, his Wolf Man screen time had to be limited anyway).

John P. Fulton, who had departed Universal after his legendary years as Special Effects Man, returned to the studio to provide the Wolf Man transformations and other supernatural flourishes to *House of Dracula*. And, as will be seen in the shooting script, Lowe scripted the climax calling for certain stock shots of the Monster from the fiery climax of *The Ghost of Frankenstein* (1942).

John Fulton, special effects pioneer

House of Dracula had some excellent vignettes.

There is Chaney's Wolf Man stalking Edelmann in the seaside cave, pouncing on the doctor, but transforming back to Talbot just before he can slay him. It is a truly frightening scene, aided by George Robinson's moody photography; and, for the last (serious) time in Universal's Wolf Man saga, we see the classic transformation from beast to man.

There is Carradine's demonic seduction of Miss O'Driscoll as she plays Moonlight Sonata at the piano; as she plays sensitively, Dracula's eyes burn into her, and the music becomes a wild, pagan-like theme - until the cross she wears upon her neck falls into view, repelling the Count's attack as the music returns to the quiet sonata. It is a richly dramatic episode, sparked by Carradine's wonderful eyes, Miss O'Driscoll's playing of fear - and an underlying theme of Faith which was such a sublime part of Universal's Horror Legacy.

Quite famous is the nightmare sequence, showing the horrors plaguing Edelmann's subconscious as Dracula's blood takes its toll on his mind and soul. Universal shot special scenes of Carradine's Dracula advancing hypnotically, Strange's Monster and Stevens' maniacal Edelmann attacking the village, and Miss Adams (sans hump) in a lovely gown, gracefully descending a staircase - and, unknowingly tempting the evil Edelmann. (This impressive vignette contained shots of Karloff's Monster from *The Bride of Frankenstein*.)

Especially exciting was the big chase scene, shot at night on Universal's old European Village set, complete with a runaway horse-and-carriage, Onslow Stevens racing about as the killer (doubled in the chase's more lively scenes by double Carey Loftin, who had doubled Karloff in the finale of *House of Frankenstein*), and the pursuing mob of villagers.

And, of course, there is the fiery climax, as the Monster - witnessing Chaney shooting Edelmann (to relieve him of his spiritual torment) - goes on a laboratory-wrecking spree. However, economy took its toll; while shooting footage of Strange in the flames, Universal completed the scene with fiery footage of Chaney's Monster from the climax of *The Ghost of Frankenstein*.

Shooting of *House of Dracula* completed Thursday, October 25, 1945. It was during production, on Sunday, October 14, 1945, that Paula Atwill gave birth to a healthy baby boy at Cedars of Lebanon Hospital. The dying actor and his wife named the infant Lionel Anthony Atwill.

Universal quickly edited *House of Dracula*. Cut from the release print was footage of little Johannes (played by Gregory Muradian, who had played Chaney's son in Strange Confession) and his Mother (Beatrice Gray); Edelmann's miracle cure of the boy's crippled leg is only referred to (by nurse Nina) in the final cut. Edgar Fairchild was musical director, adding some effectively moody music of his own (while also employing Universal's library of Hans Salter, Charles Previn and Frank Skinner horror themes). The opening title music, e.g., was the same score as heralded the credits of 1939's *Son of Frankenstein*.

On Wednesday, November 28, 1945, Universal previewed *House of Dracula* at the studio. VARIETY called the film Universal's horror special for the year, and THE HOLLYWOOD REPORTER was impressed:

"Universal holds another congress of its whole array of indestructible monsters in the Paul Malvern production called HOUSE OF DRACULA. It is a mighty good show they put up, the realms of pseudo-science interestingly invaded, and the squeamish proceedings given steady pace under the knowing direction of Erle C. Kenton. Box office expectancies should match, possibly even better, the hit grosses of the studio's previous release HOUSE OF FRANKENSTEIN...Dracula has grown taller and thinner since joining Universal's stock company and is here played by John Carradine...Lon Chaney returns as the Wolf Man, surprising only by carrying the romance in this yarn. Martha O'Driscoll is eye-arresting...Jane Adams makes a very nice thing of the hunchback nurse role entrusted to her. Glenn Strange goes on as the Frankenstein Monster, yet the greatest burden of acting is asked of Onslow

Stevens as Dr. Edelmann. He performs his chores to excellent effects...''

House of Dracula premiered at New York's Rialto Theatre on Friday, December 21, 1945, just in time for Christmas. (Ironically, the original Karloff *Frankenstein* in 1931 and *House of Frankenstein* in 1944 had also premiered in New York at Yuletide). Most of the Manhattan critics axed the melodrama, with only the NEW YORK WORLD-TELEGRAM saluting the film as good fun.

Back on the West coast, Universal released *House of Dracula* on a double bill with *The Dalton's Ride Again* (also featuring Lon Chaney and Martha O'Driscoll, along with Kent Taylor, Noah Beery Jr. and Alan Curtis) - the double feature opening Wednesday, February 6, 1946 at the Guild, United Artists, Vogue, and Fox Wilshire Theatres. Critic Lowell E. Redelings, in THE HOLLYWOOD CITIZEN-NEWS, reported of the double bill:

''...It's not high-budget film fare, nor was it meant to be. Yet, both films are so nicely done that this new bill is corking good entertainment. This reviewer enjoyed the program tremendously - and he had lots of company. If all double bills were as good as this one, there would be few complaints.''

House of Dracula closed the curtain on Universal's Frankenstein saga, abetting the studio in a $4.6 million fiscal profit for 1946. It was truly the end of an era; as the film was playing its early engagements, Universal was dropping many of its legendary attractions from the contract roster - including Lon Chaney. By the end of 1946, Universal had merged to become Universal/International, with only Deanna Durbin, Abbott and Costello, Maria Montez and a handful of other players still on the payroll.

And, in a tragic symbol of this dying era, Lionel Atwill himself died of cancer that had plagued him during *House of Dracula* - his final feature credit. The gallant, dying actor had returned to Universal City in January, 1946 to play villain Sir Eric Hazarias, sporting a panama hat, natty suit and his famous monocle in the 13- chapter serial *Lost City of the Jungle*, in which he menaced hero Russell Hayden and heroine Jane Adams (the hunchbacked Nina from *House of Dracula*). Atwill proved an inspiring professional, always on time, fully prepared, purveying his villainy all over Universal's back lot as he battled his fatal illness. Finally, on the evening of February 4, 1946, Atwill completed filming his serial death scene (perishing in an atomic blast in his getaway plane) - and left the production to face his real-life one. (Universal engaged actor George Sorel to double Atwill in the remaining footage, which the star was too sick to complete, shooting Sorel from the sides and back.) After two more months of fighting cancer, Lionel Atwill died on the evening of April 22, 1946 at his Pacific Palisades house. He left the bulk of his $250,000 estate to his wife Paula and their 6-month old son, Lionel - and left moviegoers the legacy of his wonderfully villain-

ous screen portrayals.

House of Dracula is a slick, handsome production; Erle C. Kenton's surefire direction, George Robinson's low-key photography, the Gothic sets, the gallery of fine performances. Some of the film's highlights - Carradine's ''Moonlight Sonata'' seduction of Martha O'Driscoll at the piano, the fatal carriage ride of Ludwig Stossel and Onslow Stevens in the night as Stevens' face becomes more and more bestial, the wild chase through the village and cemetery have become especially impressive vignettes in a beloved and classic series.

Yet there is a certain sadness that permeates *House of Dracula*. Perhaps it's the fact that, despite Chaney's cure as a Lycanthrope, all the major attractions perish in the film. Stevens is so compelling as the doomed Edelmann that it's truly sad to see Chaney shooting him, to release him from his horror. Even more frustrating is the fate of Jane Adams. After the lovely, former Conover model good-naturedly agreed to wear that hump, it seems overly sadistic that Nina must be strangled by Edelmann in the finale - and forced to roll over the laboratory floor and into the pit with a most unlady-like tumble!

However, the real sadness in *House of Dracula* is retrospective; the realization that we're watching beloved actors doing their last serious work in the last serious chapter of the Frankenstein saga; that we're seeing the last proficient work of Universal City's awesome talent force before its merger; that we're watching the artistry of many actors who have themselves become Hollywood folklore.

Lon Chaney went on to play in dozens of movies and scores of television appearances; besides reprising Larry Talbot in U/I's 1948 *Abbott and Costello Meet Frankenstein*, he played a werewolf in the 1959 Mexican horror film *La Casa Del Terror*, and masqueraded as the Wolf Man on the 1962 ROUTE 66 episode ''Lizard's Leg and Owlet's Wing'' (in which Lon also made up as the Mummy and his father's Hunchback, with Karloff as the Monster and Lorre as the Bogey Man). Late in his life, he conquered throat cancer, but died of a heart attack in San Clemente, California July 12, 1973. He was 67 years old, and donated his body to the University of Southern California Medical School.

John Carradine later played Dracula on the stage, on television and in several tawdry low budget films; in later years, he acted in everything from Broadway classical plays to the Academy Award-winning *Around the World in Eighty Days* (1956) to *Vampire Hookers* (1978). On Thanksgiving Day, 1988, the arthritic, 82-year old Carradine, having completed a film in Africa, visited Milan, Italy and decided to climb the 328 steps of the tower of the Duomo, the famous Gothic cathedral. He made it to the top - but collapsed, and died in a Milan hospital November 27, 1988. Sons David and Keith were at his bedside. Carradine was cremated, and his ashes scattered over the Pacific. Hailed by disciples of the Horror genre for his Dracula, Carradine always claimed he preferred Bela Lugosi's famed performance to his own. "He was the better vampire," said Carradine of Lugosi. "He had a fine pair of eyes."

Glenn Strange, after playing the Monster again in *Abbott and Costello Meet Frankenstein* settled back primarily in western fare, and spent the last 11 years of his life playing "Sam the Bartender" on CBS's GUNSMOKE. Strange died of cancer September 20, 1973, and is buried at Forest Lawn in the Hollywood Hills.

Onslow Stevens continued his character player career in such films as *Canyon Passage* (1946), *Night Has a Thousand Eyes* (1948), *Them* (1954), DeMille's *The Buccaneer* (1958), and *All the Fine Young Cannibals* (1960); in later years, he expressed regret that his showcase role in *House of Dracula* didn't win him more major film roles. His death was tragic and mysterious; on January 5, 1977, the actor died in a Van Nuys nursing home, where he was under treatment for a heart ailment - and the coroner ruled his death a murder. The veteran actor is buried at Valhalla Cemetery in North Hollywood.

Skelton Knaggs took on more grotesques in such films as *Dick Tracy Meets Gruesome* (1947), *Master Minds*

(1949) and *Blackbeard The Pirate* (1952); he died of cirrhosis of the liver April 30, 1955, at the age of only 43. Knagg's last film, Fritz Lang's *Moonfleet* (MGM, 1955), was released after his death. Knaggs is buried at Hollywood Memorial Park Cemetery.

Erle C. Kenton directed only a handful of films after *House of Dracula*; he later directed the popular television shows RACKET SQUAD, PUBLIC DEFENDER, and THE TEXAN. He died in 1980.

Finally, *House of Dracula* proved the last time Jack P. Pierce would add the celebrated makeup to the Wolf Man, Dracula and the Frankenstein Monster. Let go by Universal in 1947, the make-up wizard free-lanced, working on such films as Monogram's *Master Minds* (featuring Jane Adams, plus Glenn Strange as a giant, bearded menace named Atlas) and such television shows as FIRESIDE THEATRE, YOU ARE THERE and MR. ED. Pierce died July 19, 1968, at the age of 79, and is buried at Forest Lawn, Glendale. Boris Karloff, from his home in England, sent a beautiful floral wreath to convey his respects for the man he always hailed as a genius.

Today, Universal City, California is the nation's third largest tourist attraction. In 1992, the attractions there

Universal Studios' Hollywood European Village - Home of the Classic Universal Monsters - part original - partly rebuilt - as it can be seen today on the Universal Tour

boasted a ride past the wrath of King Kong, a Wild West stuntman show, a newly added Backdraft attraction, a ride through the world of E.T., an exhibit of trained animals, a live Conan the Barbarian show, and much more - along with the tram ride over Universal's historic back lot.

When visiting the Universal Studios Hollywood Tour, the tram makes a reverential stop on the old European Village set - where, 60 years ago, the Hollywood peasants first lit their torches to hunt Frankenstein's Monster. Fire has attacked the old village a number of times since the 1960s, but, like the Monster, the set has risen like the Phoenix from the ashes, and stills stands, a little shrine to the folklore and magic created by Universal's Classic Monster films.

And as the last tram car putters away, the sun sets behind the mountains, and the moon rises into the night sky, one can imagine the ghosts that return to that hallowed old set - and the pride the ghosts feel in the most beloved Horror Films ever created.

Universal's new Classic Monster logo

HOUSE OF DRACULA

Studio: Universal
Producer: Paul Malvern
Executive Producer: Joe Gershenson
Director: Erle C. Kenton
Screenplay: Edward T. Lowe
    (based on a story by George Bricker &
    Dwight V. Babcock)
Additional material (uncredited)
    by Edward S. Laine
Cinematographer: George Robinson
Film Editor: Russell Schoengarth
Art Directors: John B. Goodman &
    Martin Obzina
Sound Director: Bernard B. Brown
    (Jess Moulin, Technician)
Set Decorators: Russell A. Gausman
    & Arthur D. Leddy
Gowns: Vera West
Makeup Artist: Jack P. Pierce
Hair Stylist: Carmen Dirigo
Special Photography Effects: John P. Fulton
Musical Director: Edgar Fairchild
Assistant Director: Ralph Slosser
Completion Date: October 25, 1945
Premiere: Rialto Theatre,
New York City, December 21, 1945

THE PLAYERS

Lawrence Talbot........................Lon Chaney
Count Dracula.......................John Carradine
Miliza.............................Martha O'Driscoll
Inspector Holtz......................Lionel Atwill
Dr. Franz Edelmann.................Onslow Stevens
The Frankenstein Monster.............Glenn Strange
Nina...................................Jane Adams
Ziegfried............................Ludwig Stossel
Steinmuhl..........................Skelton Knaggs
Brahms..........................Joseph E. Bernard
Villager............................Dick Dickinson
Gendarmes...........Fred Cordova, Carey Harrison
Villager...........................Harry Lamont
Johannes.......................Gregory Muradian*
Mother..............................Beatrice Gray*
Double for Stevens....................Carey Loftin
Stand-In for Chaney................Walt De Palma
Stand-In for Carradine..............Arthur W. Stern

* Footage Deleted

Signatures

Luck
Lon Chaney

Lon Chaney Jr.

Glenn Strange

Glenn Strange

with good wishes
John Carradine

John Carradine

Jack Pierce

Jack Pierce

Martha O'Driscoll

Martha O'Driscoll

Lionel Atwill

Lionel Atwill

Jane Adams

Jane Adams

Hans J. Salter

Hans Salter (Composer)

Frank Skinner

Frank Skinner (Composer)

Onslow Stevens

Onslow Stevens

Tad and Dennis Devine with Glenn Strange in his completed monster makeup

Makeup & Special Effects Department

Director Erle C. Kenton and Camera/ Effects man Frank Heisler discuss a camera distortion screen with John Carradine. Kenton's Universal monster films were the first to show the transformation of Dracula into a bat on-screen, by this method.

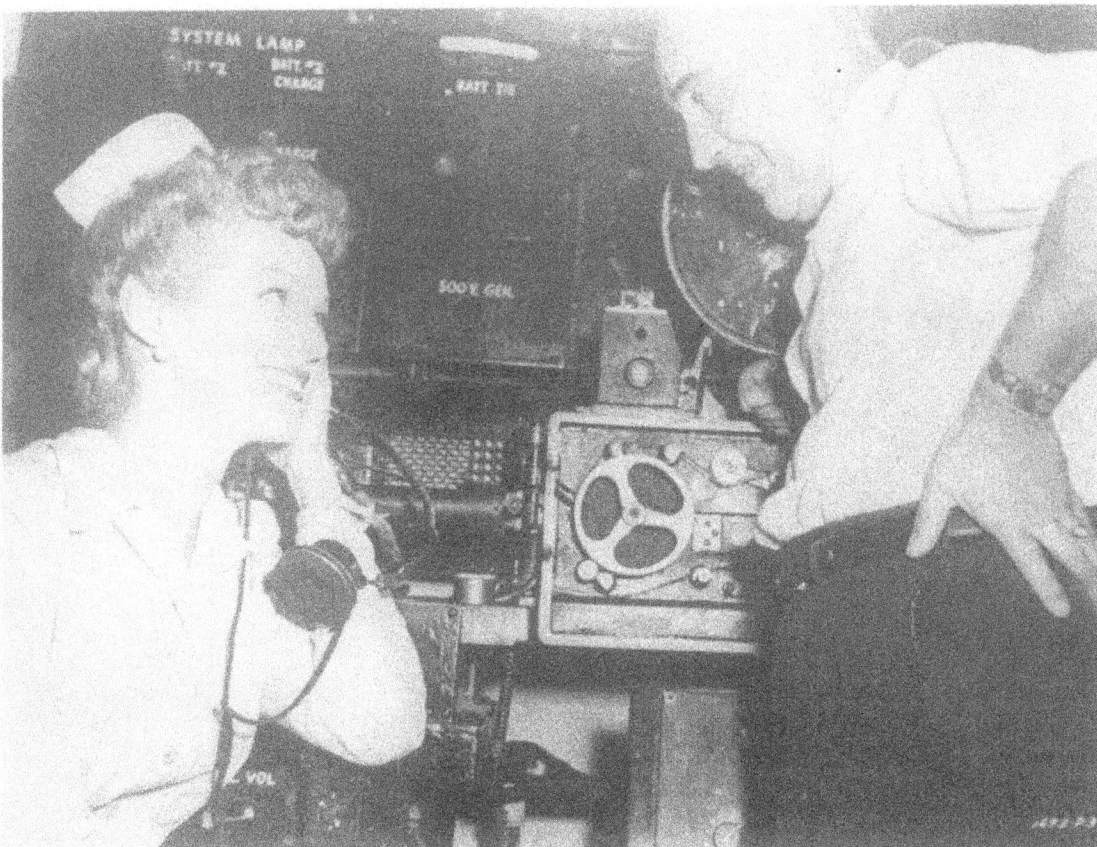

Martha O'Driscoll listens to the dialog sound track on the location mastering recorders. The sound man is Jimmy Masterson.

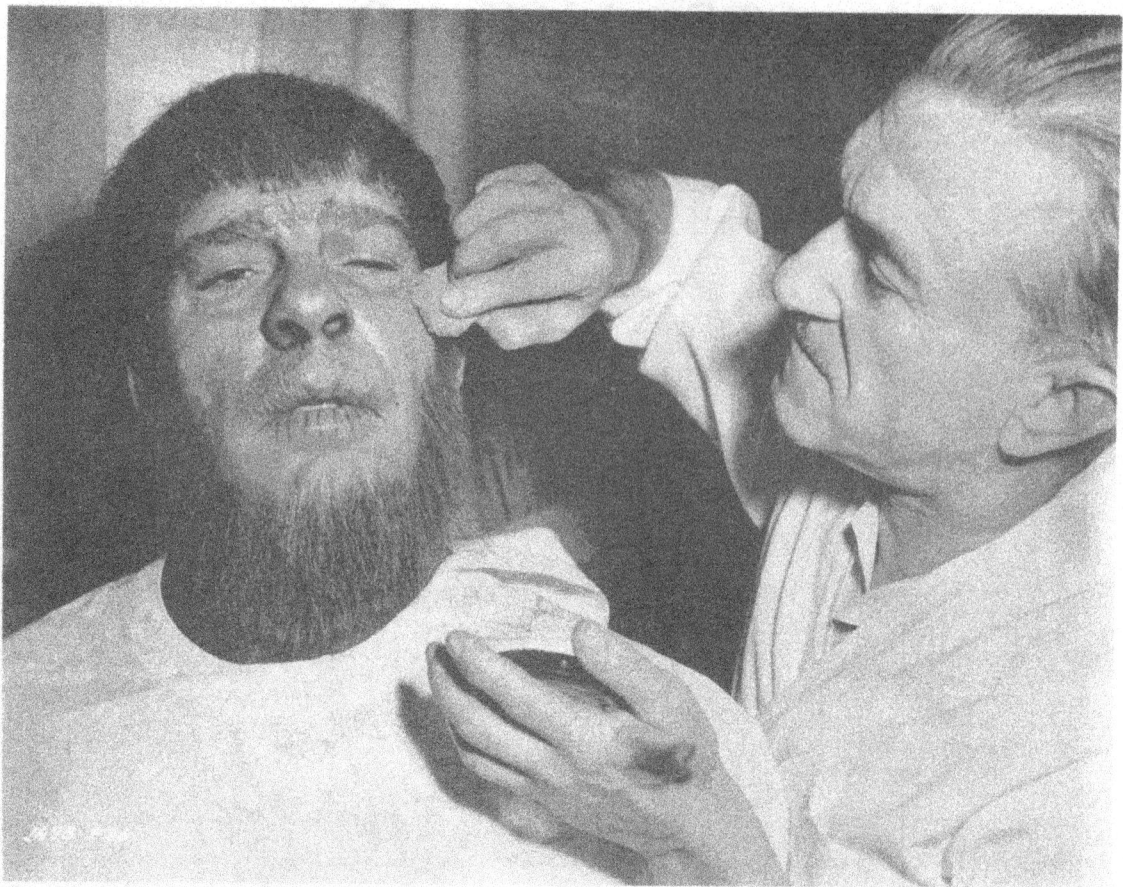

Jack Pierce applies Chaney's Wolf Man makeup for the transformation scene.

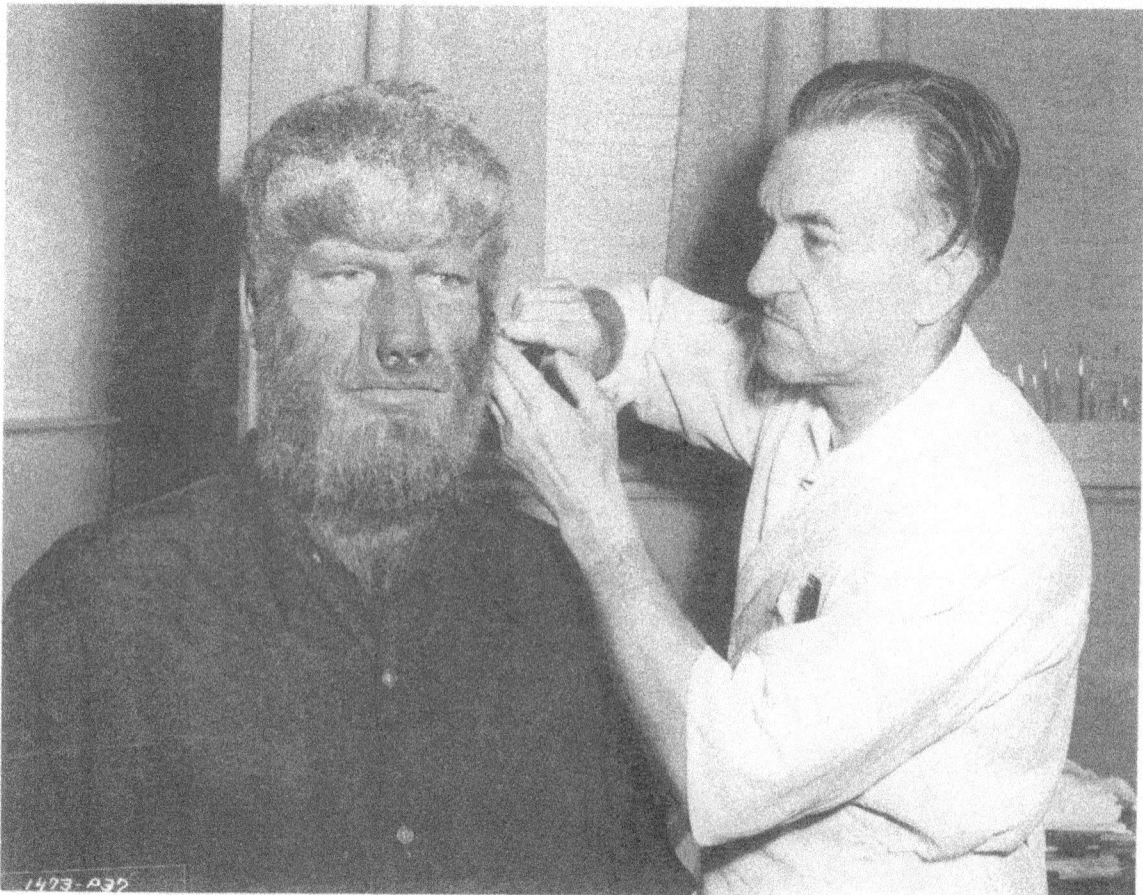

Chaney in the completed Pierce creation - the nose and cheeks were bright red which registered as brown in the camera.

Jane Adams and Martha O'Driscoll pose with Chaney in the finished Wolf Man Makeup.

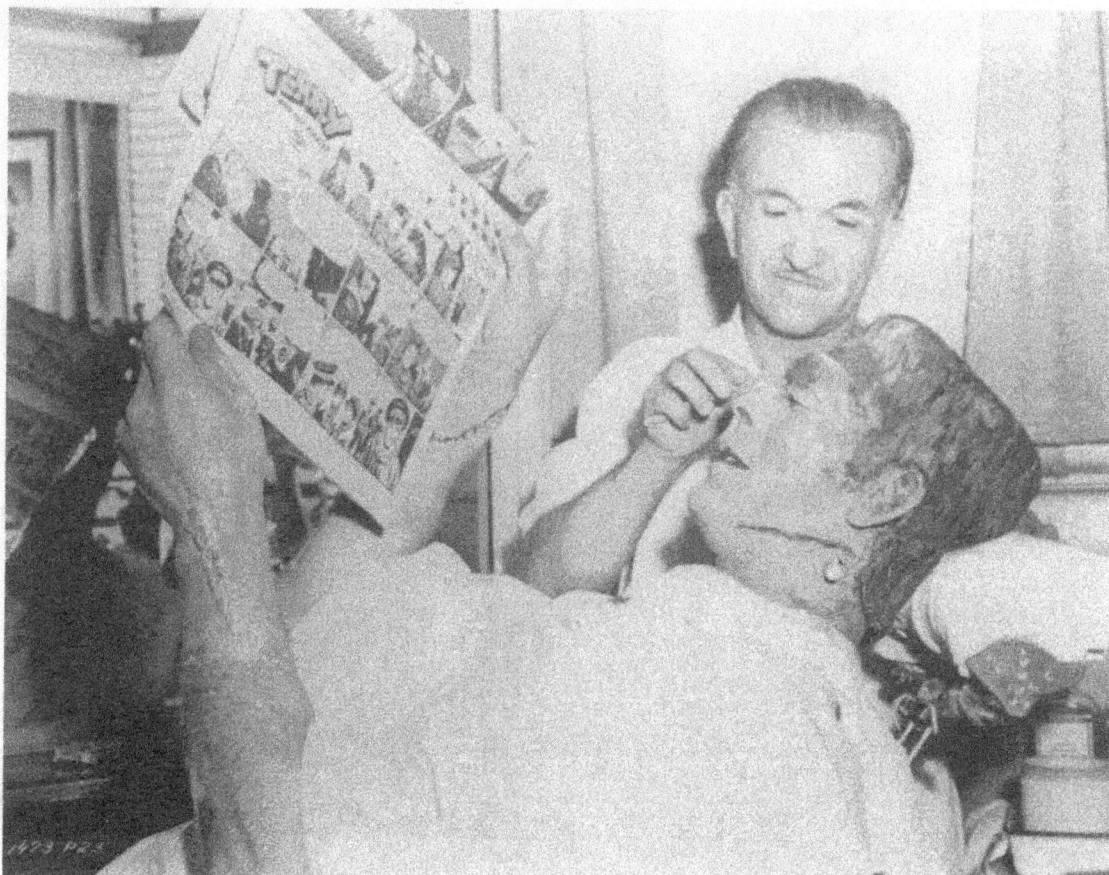

Glenn Strange goes through the 4 hour ordeal of being made up as the Frankenstein Monster.

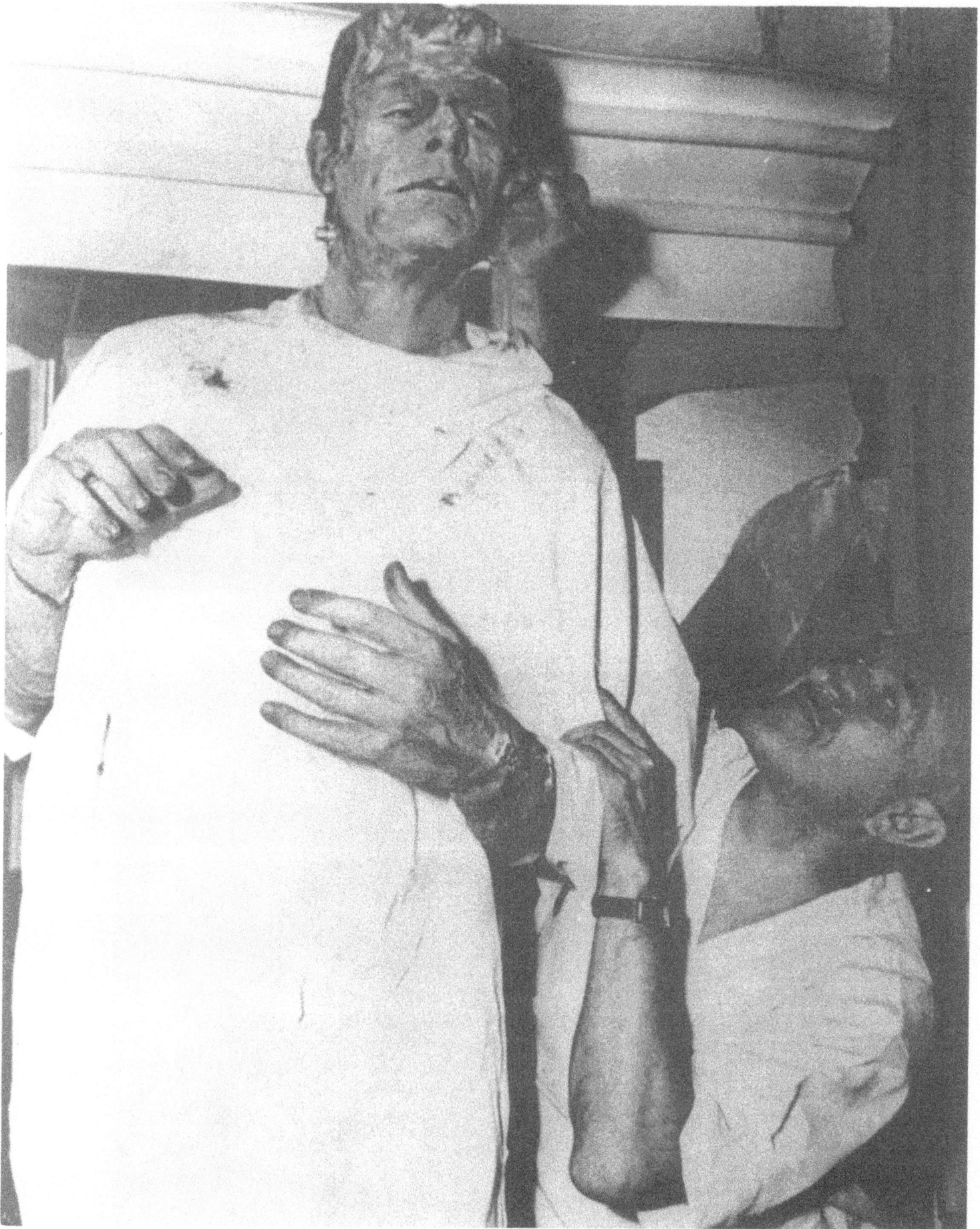

Strange, at 7'2" patiently waits for Pierce to apply the head-piece and the collodion scars with spirit gum.

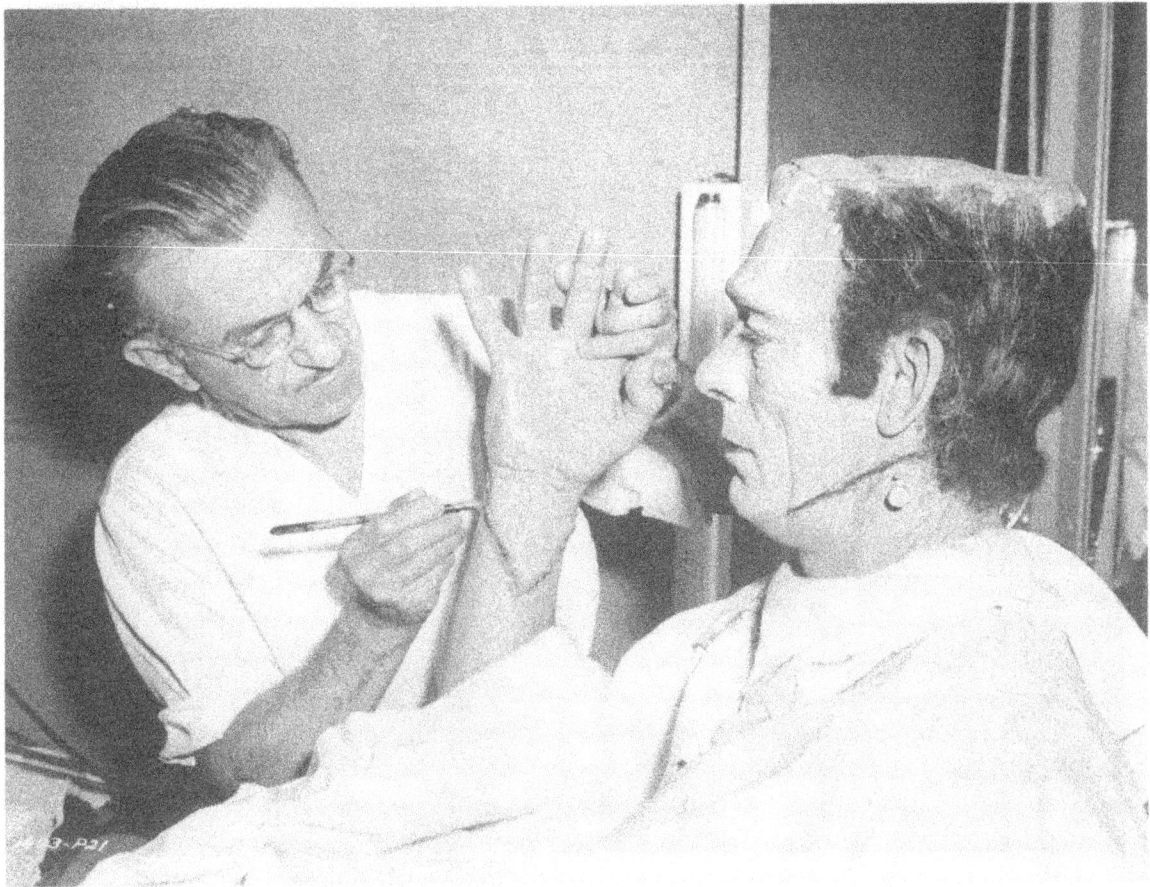

(Above) Pierce's attention to detail in the last time that he would make up an actor in his classic creation (Below) the final grey-green coating is applied to Strange.

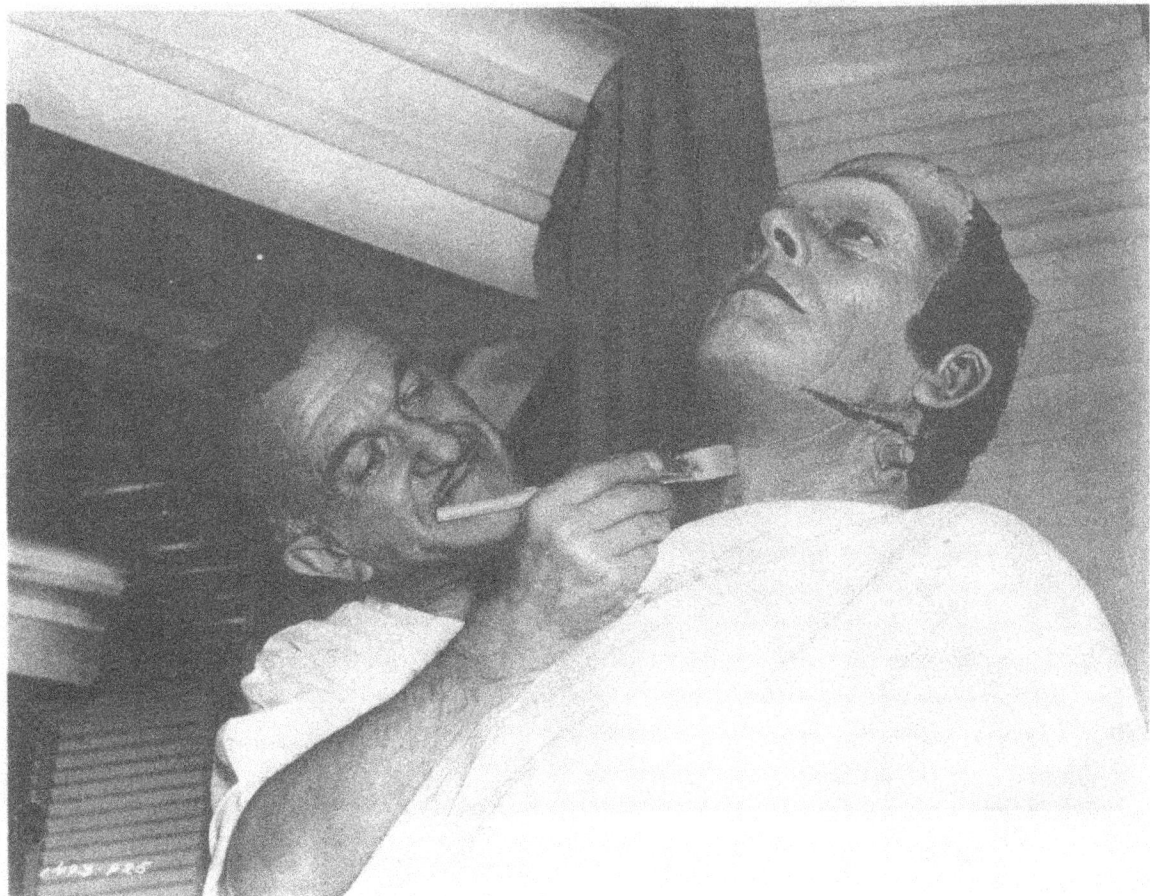

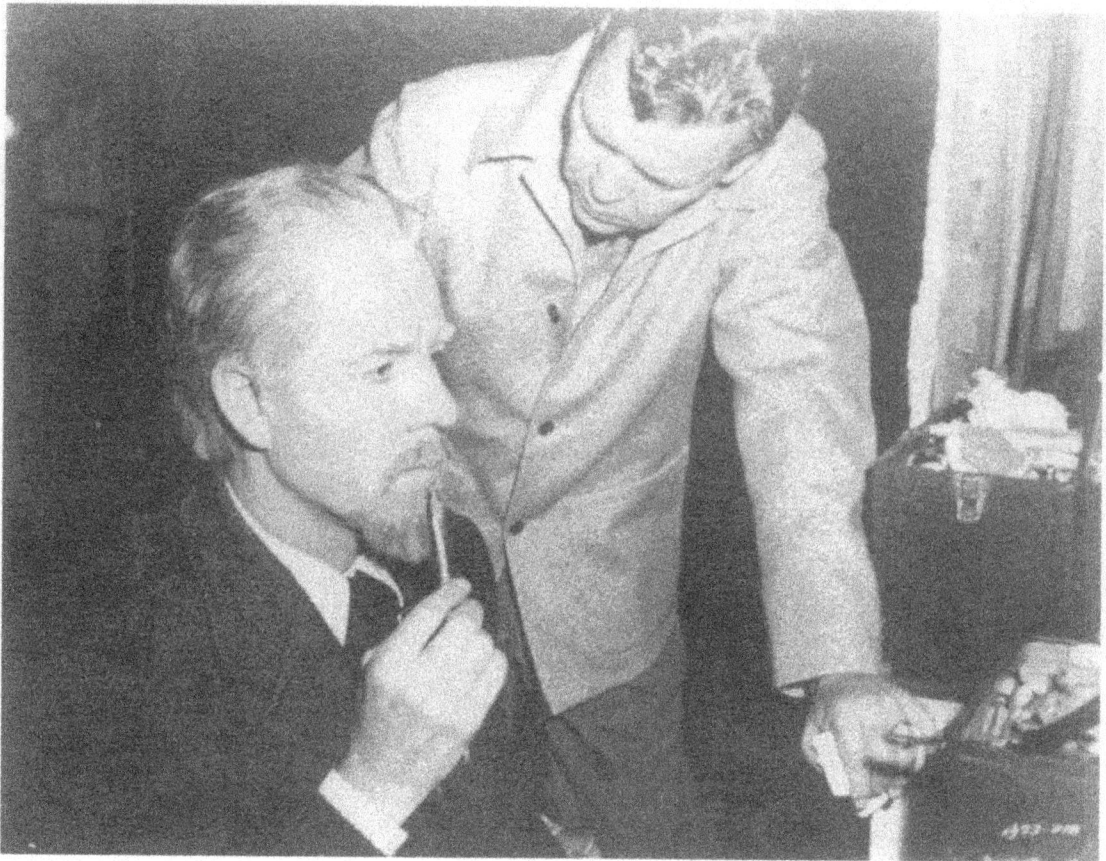

Onslow Stevens touches up his makeup while discussing a scene.

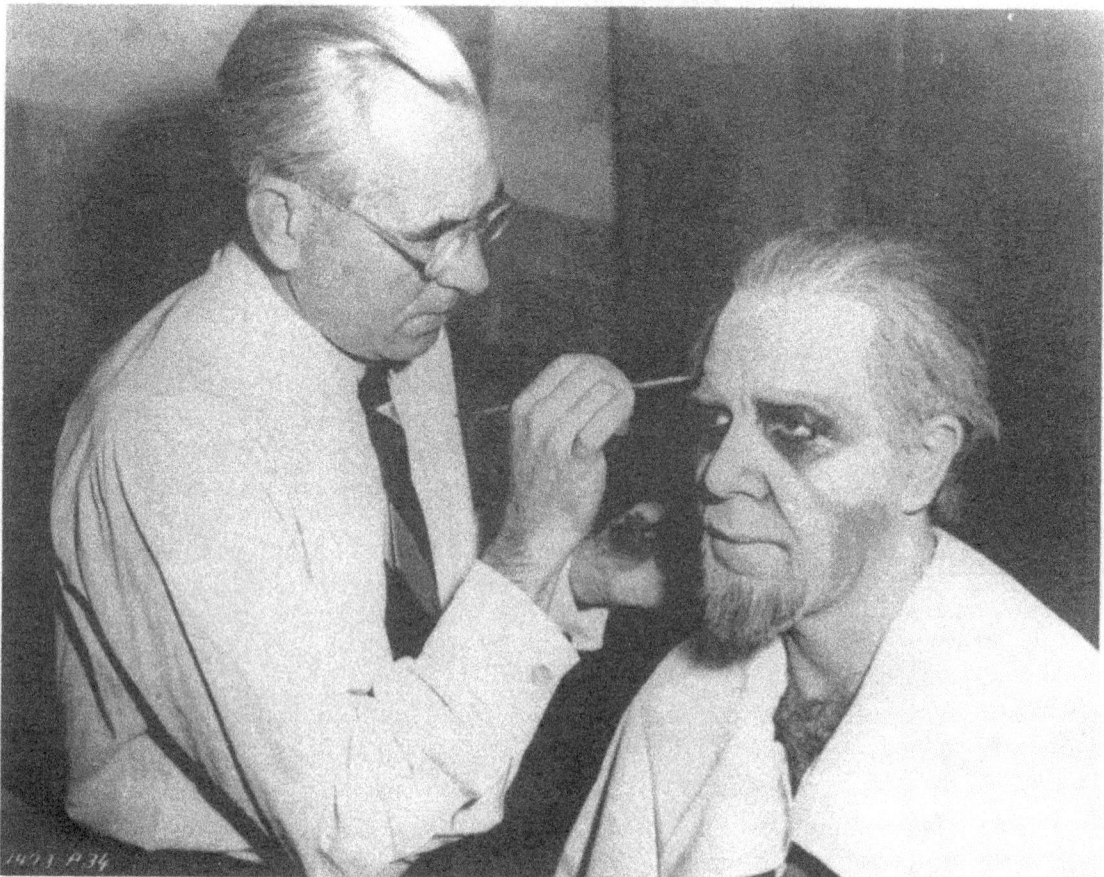

Joe Hadley, again applying the evil Doctor Edelmann makeup on Onslow Stevens

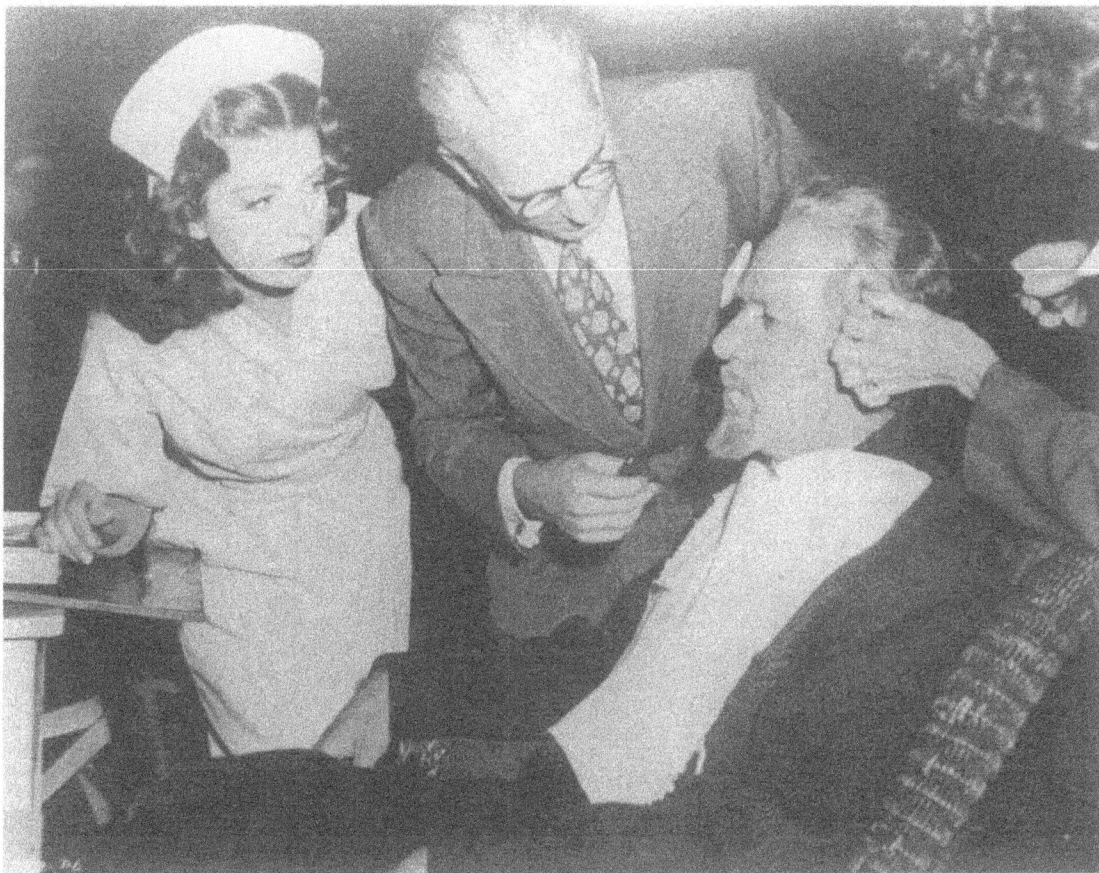

Joe Hadley inspects Stevens makeup as Jane Adams looks on. Note the hands of the special effects assistant on the right holding the thin wire attached to Steven's head to hold him in place for the transformation scene as Dracula's blood contamination turns him into a madman.

Jane Adams and Director Kenton pose for publicity shots in Dr. Edelmann's lab.

Gregory Muradian (right) and Gordon Barber (his stand-in) sit on Martha O'Driscoll's lap during shooting. Gregory's part as a young man healed by Dr. Edelmann was cut from the final release.

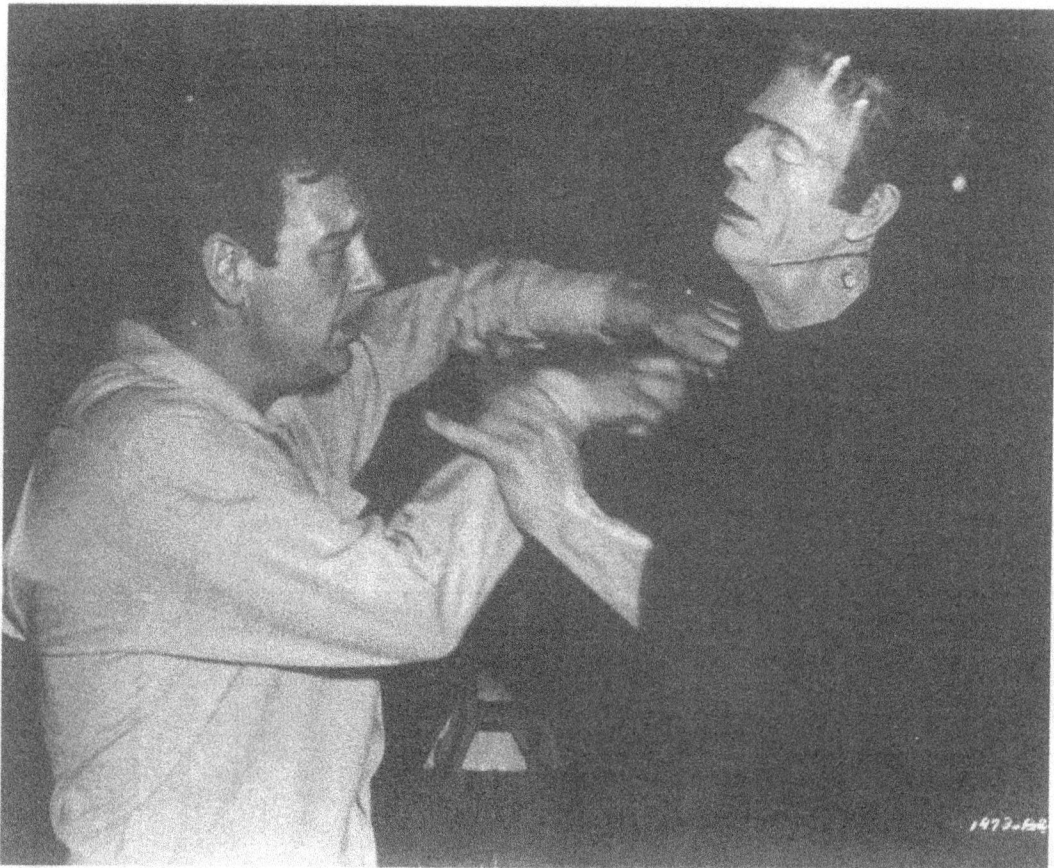

Lon Chaney Jr. and Glenn Strange rehearsing the climax of the film - (The studio publicity caption reads that Chaney was helping Strange with his costume.)

Martha O'Driscoll adds her name with Universal Stars, Preston Foster, Peter Coe, Andy Devine, Dana Andrews, Deanna Durbin and others on a giant blow up of a Victory War Bond to celebrate the end of WW II.

Jane Adams receives a surprise visit from her Brother-in-law, Infantryman Lieut. Joseph Turnage - Everybody gets in the act!

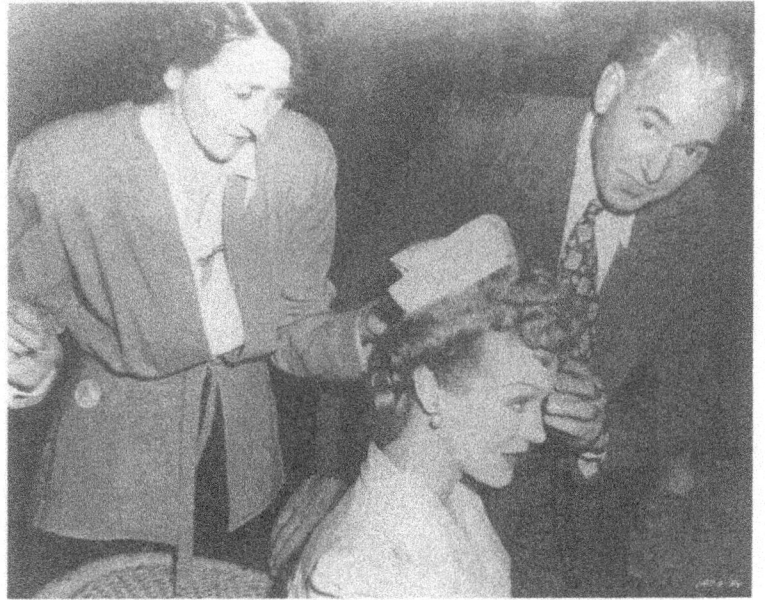

Hairdresser Alta Hitchcock and Make-up man Joe Hadley prepare Martha O'Driscoll as the Vampire's victim.

Lon Chaney, in his fourth Wolf Man film is aided by his stunt double Walter DePalma. Their friendship spanned several decades.

John Carradine and his stand-in /stunt double, Arthur W. Stern

Oslow Stevens and his stunt double Carey Loftin are difficult to tell-apart even in a still photograph.

A Last Look at the original Backlot sets used in the Classic Universal Monster Films

From the original 1923 Hunchback of Notre Dame *to the 1955* Man of a Thousand Faces, *these sets were the home of not only the monsters and science fiction films but also Sherlock Holmes, Mysteries and War films. Most were destroyed by fire in the 1960s.*

Much of the original European Village remains today, including the Court of Miracles and can be seen on the Universal Hollywood Tour. Other sets have been rebuilt using the original blueprints.

" WOLFMAN VS. DRACULA "

by

BERNARD SCHUBERT

NOVEMBER 30, 1944

THE CAMERA shows the Bat caught in the branches of the
tree, unable to get at his victim, who, badly shaken
but unhurt, get C their feet and continue on PAST
CAMERA, WHICH HOLDS ON THE BAT, struggling in the branches.

193   CLOSE SHOT - GARDEN - NEAR THE FOUNTAIN

As Talbot and Yvonne, exhausted, shaken and frightened,
are just about to reach the fountain, Yvonne, notices
his face -

                    YVONNE
                  (panting)
            Your face is bleeding terribly...

She looks toward the Fountain and water. He divines
her thought -

                    TALBOT
                 (earnestly
                  concerned)
            We can't stop now, Yvonne...

                    YVONNE
              (actually for his
               sake, not her
               own)
            Please LARRY... Just for a
            second... I'm exhausted...
            I....

He turns to see if the Bat is still coming after them.
She crosses to the Fountain, takes her handkerchief,
wets it, and crosses back to him to mop his face with
it. As she does, while neither of them realise it,
the Bat again files INTO SCENE... With a terrific
power the Bat dives down at their heads and heads
Then Talbot down to his knees in a stunning blow.
to attack her. With the Bat between Yvonne and himself,
Talbot still on his knees fires point-blank. For a
fraction of a second, it looks as though he might have
hit Yvonne, who falters with the shot, when the Bat
falls to the ground, in a swooping movement.

CAMERA ZOOMS TO THE GROUND near the Fountain where the
Bat has turned into the figure of Dr. Mule.

                                        CONTINUED

Script Development
From *Wolf Man vs. Dracula* to *House of Dracula*
by Philip Riley

While production of *Frankenstein Meets the Wolf Man* was underway, Universal began to prepare for another sequel. But the idea of another Frankenstein sequel without Boris Karloff was not well received. Since Lon Chaney Jr. and Bela Lugosi were currently on the lot, the logical step after the Wolf Man met Frankenstein would be to have him meet Dracula. The project was given to director Ford Beebe.

Beebe, born on November 26, 1888 in Grand Rapids, Michigan, started his film career around 1920. His main concentration was on low-budget westerns and action pictures.

In 1932 he directed countless films for Mascot, Columbia and Republic. At Universal he co-directed *Flash Gordon's Trip to Mars* and *Buck Rogers*. His association with Paul Malvern had been a long one and considering his record of low-budget, but highly entertaining films, it might have been a highlight in the 40s Horror film revival by Universal. Some of his other films related to fantasy and monsters included, *The Phantom Creeps, The Green Hornet, Flash Gordon Conquers the Universe in 1938;* at Disney Studios he directed the Beethoven "Pastoral Symphony" segment of *Fantasia;* 1942, *Night Monster, The Son of Dracula* (as producer and 2nd Unit director) and in 1943 *The Invisible Man's Revenge*.

Beebe had been given the assignment to follow up on the anticipated success of *Frankenstein Meets the Wolf Man* and so he had Bernard Schubert hired to write the script and story. The result was "WOLF MAN VS. DRACULA." A first draft of the script was turned in May 19, 1944. Bela Lugosi was to play Count Dracula, under the name Dr. A. Kula, and Lon Chaney was to revive his Wolf Man role.

The setting was Transylvania. The opening credits called for "Bach's Tocatta & Fugue in Dm." In the local hospital a Dr. Ziska was capturing the attention of the medical world by his successful removal of a bullet from the head of a man found by two local peasants. The man had been found with a rotting skeleton and brought to the hospital where it was discovered that he was still alive. Reporters gathered around the hospital where they compared their headlines:

"BURIED ALIVE FOR THIRTY-FIVE YEARS"

"STRANGE CASE THAT HAS BAFFLED SCIENCE HAS COME TO LIGHT WITH THE UNEARTHING OF TWO FIGURES"

As the patient revives from the operation he is found to be raving. He begs the doctor to kill him. It is Larry Talbot. The Doctor orders a sedative and leaves the man with his assistants to attend a conference. He returns that evening just as the moon is rising and decides to check in on his patient.

[Editor's note: o.s. = Off Scene
MED. = Medium Shot
THRU = Through
INT = Interior
EXT = Exterior
TRUCKING SHOT = Camera is moved along track
PAN = Camera is stationary but turns slowly within the scene on a camera tripod

The following excerpt from the first draft screenplay shows why the censors thought the picture was considered "not-suitable" for the 1940s audience.

> DR. ZISKA
> It is better maybe you rest now . . .
> We can talk plenty later . . .

He [Talbot] turns away, recrossing the beam of moonlight. Talbot, following with his eyes, becomes conscious of the beam of moonlight streaming into room. CAMERA PANS HIS LOOK AND FOLLOWS THE MOONLIGHT TO THE IRON-BARRED WINDOWS.

7. EFFECT SHOT - SHOOTING THRU BARRED WINDOW OVER GABLED ROOF TOPS TOWARD THE FULL MOON IN THE HEAVENS ABOVE.

8. INT. HOSPITAL ROOM - MED. TRUCKING SHOT

CAMERA PULLS AWAY FROM WINDOW, disclosing Talbot leaning out of bed, his face bright in the moonlight, while Dr. Ziska, standing in the semi-darkness, studies him curiously. WHEN CAMERA PANS AWAY FROM THEM, TO NURSE, HER BACK TO CAMERA, busy over a table on the other side of the room, TRUCKING UP CLOSER, THE NOSEY CAMERA TRIES TO TAKE A PEEK OVER HER SHOULDER, only to SEE her preparing a basin of some warm water, presumably to sponge the patient.

Suddenly HEARING the SOUND of movement o.s. and behind her, she hardly looks up when she sees ON THE WALL IN FRONT OF HER, the shadow of Talbot leaping from his bed and grabbing the Doctor by the throat, as we HEAR from o.s. the brief sound of a struggle . . .she turns quickly to face CAMERA and before she can even make a move, from o.s. we HEAR the SOUND of a blood-congealing cry of a human in agonized pain, and the dull THUD of a body hitting the floor . . . .Upon the Nurse's face is written such a look of horror that she can not even give voice to her alarm . . . Instinctively, she shrinks back, at the growl of the infuriated beast. As she stands there, we SEE across her face, the MOVING SHADOW of the Wolf Man's head. He holds his position ominously for a second, then starts on his way toward the window rear o.s. . . . . Her eyes hypnotically stare and follow his direction toward the o.s. window . . . Then there is a resounding CRASH of glass followed by another animal growl of fury, as he tugs at the bars . . . They evidently give way, as clouds of dust COME INTO SCENE, with the SOUND of mortar and brick falling . . . THE CAMERA TRUCKING BACK TO WIDER ANGLE shows the window is smashed, the shattered glass is scattered all around . . . .The heavy iron bars guarding the rear window are twisted and torn out of the wall, while on the floor near the empty bed, lying in a pool of blood is the eminent Dr. Ziska, his jugular vein gouged and his throat bestially lacerated. The nurse, Sister Elizabeth, is still speechless, when attracted by the screams and commotion, there rushes into the room the excited Superintendent, Dr. Kleber, followed by hospital attendants, foreign correspondents, a Nurse and others.

The first draft script continues with Larry Talbot being discovered by Yvonne. He is sitting on a tree stump holding his head in his hands. She takes pity on him and offers food and drink at the home of her father Anatole.

Anatole is the village executioner and welcomes any guest in his home as he and his daughter are shunned by the locals. Talbot asks Anatole to free him of the curse of the werewolf, but Anatole refuses. He suggests that Talbot seek help at the castle of Dr. Kula. Yvonne is a part-time housekeeper for the Doctor.

There is a knock at the door and Domenica, Dr. Kula's, daughter enters. She immediately senses something occult about Talbot and invites him to the Castle. Outside Dr. Kula is waiting in a carriage. He recognizes Talbot but stays in the shadows of the carriage interior, explaining that he has lost the use of his legs and is confined to a wheel chair. Domenica jumps onto the drivers seat and guides the mysterious carriage toward the castle, while Talbot tries to shake off the hypnotic spell that Domenica has already begun to weave over him.

Talbot and Yvonne begin to fall in love. But Talbot has an ulterior motive. He takes Yvonne to the village priest and they are married.

Anatole confronts Talbot and he is told that although Talbot is fond of Yvonne, he only married her to force Anatole to kill him, for he has already seen the pentagram in the hand of Yvonne and the werewolf always kills the one it loves the most.

The remaining script is full of special effects involving Dracula as a giant bat in a life and death struggle with the Wolf Man. Magic, supernatural elements and the occult play a big part in the plot. Bela Lugosi's part takes up most of the remaining action with the giant bat sequence's specifically designed for stunt man Eddie Parker as Lugosi was now over 60 years old.

The studio executives loved the idea and immediately began budgeting the film, but then the unexpected happened. Boris Karloff finally agreed to come back to Universal for a two picture deal. The agreement was reached on March 30, 1944 unknown to Lugosi and to Ford Beebe. The two pictures were *Destiny*, later to become *House of Frankenstein* and *The Climax*. *Wolf Man vs. Dracula* was pushed back to allow for Karloff's schedule. The two productions existed simultaniously for a short time, *House of Frankenstein* having begun shooting on April 4th 1944. But then the delays began on *Wolf Man vs. Dracula*. First, the reaction to Bela Lugosi's editorially butchered Frankenstein's monster, who was to speak with Ygor's voice,* was not well received. Also there were negotiation troubles over Lugosi's contract and finally the Censor's Bureau made so many demands that the project was again stalled.

The rushes of John Carradine's Dracula in *House of Frankenstein* gave them an option. So, by the time production was to start on "Wolf Man vs. Dracula" in the fall of 1944, negotiations with Lugosi ended and John Carradine was again optioned for the part.

A final shooting script dated November 30, 1944 was turned in by Bernard Schubert. Producer Malvern had all of the cuts made as specified by Joseph Breen of the Motion Picture Producers and Distributors censors office.

The second draft final was a tighter script with minor

variations. It opened with the reporters being led to the bodies of the supposedly dead Larry Talbot and the skeleton of the gypsy girl by a local peasant. Dr. Ziska is not killed by the Wolf Man and Dracula's name is changed from Dr. Kula to Dr. Draulac.

Dr. Draulac is anxious to marry the young and beautiful Yvonne. When Anatole refuses, Dracula changes into a bat and flies to Yvonne's bedroom, puts her under a spell and is about to have her remove her crucifix, when Larry Talbot enters and Dracula leaves. The seeds of the final shooting script are present in this draft, but in crude form.

Talbot still goes to Dracula for treatment to cure his lycanthropy, but instead finds a room full of occult books, one on Vampires and Werewolves.

Dracula then frames Larry Talbot, who now has the police from Transylvania closing in on him for the murder of the police surgeon at the beginning of the script. He (Dracula) transforms himself into a Werewolf and attacks a local villager, while Talbot is not far away.

With the Police after him, Talbot goes to Anatole and Yvonne and tells them about Dracula. He gives them the book on Vampires and Werewolves and sets out for Dracula's castle to destroy him.

All scenes involving the giant bat were eliminated in this version and Dracula meets his end in the usual stake-thru-the-heart method by Talbot's hand. Screenwriter Schubert again got caught by the censors and they demanded the removal of lines like "There is a SOUND as of a STAKE BEING JAMMED THROUGH A SOLID BODY accompanied by an EAR SPLIT-TING SCREAM. . ."

Dracula's tomb is destroyed by Talbot, pulling a support beam away from the undercasement of the tomb. And what of Talbot and Yvonne?

As a mob of gendarmes and villagers approach the castle, they find Yvonne being revived by Anatole. At that point the moon rises and Talbot, struggling with the beast-man transformation in the rubble, attacks the mob. The following 8 pages of script are some of the most violent Wolf Man scenes ever written. The Wolf Man rips apart half the local peasants and police in various rooms of Dracula's castle during a mad hunt and destroy chase scene. He is finally about to kill the chief of police, when Yvonne rushes up the steps to him and in the manner of *Werewolf of London*, he almost regains his human soul when he sees Yvonne. This is just enough time for Anatole to finish him off with a silver bullet. And the script ends with Talbot saying to Anatole,

"Thanks friend, now I can rest in - -"

Again the censors demanded cuts and so the production was cancelled and the script put away in the vaults for almost 6 months.

Then the box office receipts of *House of Frankenstein*, released in December of 1944, started to show promise. Producer Malvern went back into the files and hired the writer of *House of Frankenstein*, Edward T. Lowe, to rework the script. Ford Bebee was now involved in other projects and so Erle C. Kenton took over as Director.

On April 13, 1945 Lowe's first Sequence outline reads almost like the finished script of *House of Dracula*, as presented in this volume. The new element was the addition of the Frankenstein monster. Lowe, not wanting to take chances of

*[See MagicImage - Universal Filmscript Series Volume 3 - *Son of Frankenstein*, Volume 4 - *The Ghost of Frankenstein* and Volume 5 - *Frankenstein Meets the Wolf Man* for an in-depth study of the character continuity]

having the production cancelled again, because of the name being associated with the previous production, took advantage of a long running joke in the writer's building at Universal. The writers knew that the producers did not know much about what went on on the backlot during shooting.

To give the producers something to make them think that they were being creative, they would call the picture *Destiny*, expecting the producers to say, "That's a lousy title!" The producers would then change it to something else and feel like they contributed something to the success of the film.

Two days later Lowe delivered the first treatment. This is the first time that Nina is made a hunchback. Other changes just detail the previously quoted Sequence Outline of April 13. A short synopsis of the final script:

The Doctor travels to Transylvania at the request of Dracula. He arrives, much like Jonathan Harker in the original "Dracula." Fog shrouded mountain passes, ghost-like mists, and a meeting at the Borgo Pass. The Doctor is met by Dracula, disguised as a coachman, with the exception of his "red glowing eyes." Dracula and Doctor Edelmann make an agreement to cure Dracula of his blood lust. Part of the agreement is that Dracula must be staked through the heart and revived by the removal of the stake when he arrives at the Doctor's clinic. Dracula agrees and dematerializes into a skeleton to allow the Doctor to insert the stake without too much blood and gore. Doctor returns to Vasaria to await Dracula's arrival. The contamination of Dr. Edelmann's blood is an accident in this treatment. Nina accidently breaks the electrical connection to the transfusion pump and when she reconnects it, it is reversed.

Larry Talbot now arrives and asks for his chance at being cured of his werewolf curse. When he is told to wait, the action follows the final shooting script, which includes the discovery of the Frankenstein monster with Dr. Neumann's skeleton in the underground cave.

Dr. Edelmann begins to feel the effects of Dracula's blood. He watches Dracula closely and after finding him commanding Miliza to remove her crucifix, Edelmann goes to his study and prays over a wooded ash stake. At dawn he goes to Dracula's coffin in the basement, drives the stake through his heart and burns the coffin. He tells Miliza and Nina that Dracula lost faith in his ability to cure him and so he departed.

Talbot is cured of his lycanthropy by an on-screen operation where we see the Doctor reshaping his skull after applying the calcium softening spores.

Gradually the blood of Dracula takes over the good side of the Doctor and he sets about to revive the Frankenstein Monster.

Nina tries to stop him, but she is carried off to the lower levels. Talbot and Miliza are in pursuit. Finally Talbot chases them into the caves where Dr. Edelmann and the Monster are backed into a dead end. Dr. Edelmann has changed into a raving psychopath with the physical features described as between Mr. Hyde ("Dr. Jekyll and Mr. Hyde" by Robert Lewis Stevenson) and "a thing that is neither man nor beast, but obviously a creation of horror whose existence must be ended, now."

A battle commences in which the Monster tears stalactites down from the cave and throws them at Talbot. The Monster breaks a supporting stalagmite and its mating stalactite hanging from the cavern's roof and this releases a hidden underground spring. Water begins to pour into the cave as the monster and the mad-man pursue Talbot.

"Pursued by the monster and Edelmann, Talbot plunges through the quickly rising water, dashing toward the exit to the corridor as the whirling torrents now assume the proportions of a whirlpool, a maelstrom of force which eats into the bases of the columns that support the cavern's roof."

Talbot bars the doors of the laboratory while Miliza rushes up and brings the other patients in the Doctor's clinic to a safe point away from the castle.

Just as the monster and Dr. Edelmann break through the door the water has undermined the castle to such a point that the floor gives way and - "in mute horror as with a rending crash that might be the death-cry of a dying giant, the castle crumbles and disappears into the gaping maw of the earth which opens to receive it."

Lowe rewrote the screenplay 3 more times, borrowing scenes from earlier films such as the musical piece, which changes from a peaceful melody to an eerie evil theme, much like the scene from *Dracula's Daughter* (1936). The transformation of Henry Hull into the werewolf and the violent reaction of a cat were lifted from *Werewolf of London*. During the rewrites, someone in production sent a memo to Lowe, that they "did not like the title *Destiny* and it should be more like the previous monster films - like *House of Frankenstein* - how about changing the name to *House of Dracula*?" To Lowe's relief, the trick worked and the title stuck. All written material in the files indicate that it must have been known that this would be the last of the Classic Universal Monster films for the present studio administration. Budget cuts demanded the change in ending from the cave to the "stock shots" of the monsters destruction and Dracula's true death was finalized by not only having a stake driven through his heart, but his head cut off, his coffin burnt and the ashes scattered. (In just a few short decades, Count Dracula's reaction to the sacred symbols has gone from one of fear to indifference. Lugosi's Dracula, fled the room when Van Helsing held up a crucifix. Today Dracula just stamps his foot and the crucifix bursts into flames.)

As an interesting note, *House of Dracula* was considered for a Technicolor release. There is reference to the various Technicolor shadings that could be used for certain scenes. However, no record of agreement with Technicolor for this production could be located, nor are there any lab records that would indicate that any testing was done in Technicolor.

The unfilmed history of Universal is almost as legendary as its classic films. "Wolf Man Vs. Dracula" is just one of many scripts which were never filmed in their original form. Other notable ones include:

James Whale's treatments of "Bride of Frankenstein" & "The Invisible Man"
Robert Florey's script for "Frankenstein"
The complete Louis Bromfield's "Dracula"
Robert Florey's "The Wolf Man (written for Boris Karloff)
R. C. Sheriff's script for James Whale's version of "Dracula's Daughter" to star Bela Lugosi
and many long lost versions of classic films of what might have been . . . or were produced in alternate forms.

On the following pages we present the original pressbook for
House of Dracula
which was distributed to theater owners
for publicity purposes in 1945

SUPER
SHOCKER
OF
THEM
ALL!
Universal
Presents
HOUSE OF DRACULA
Copyright 1945
Universal Pictures
Co., Inc.

Universal's Super-Sequel to Record-Wrecking "House of Frankenstein"!

THE MIGHTIEST MONSTERS OF ALL TIME...

All Together!

The Same BIG "SELL"... Geared to Even BIGGER GROSSES! Sock 'em with a SUPER-SHOCK CAMPAIGN!

HOUSE OF DRACULA

with

LON CHANEY   MARTHA O'DRISCOLL
JOHN CARRADINE   LIONEL ATWILL

Onslow Stevens   Glenn Strange   Jane Adams   Ludwig Stossel

Original Screenplay by Edward T. Lowe • Directed by ERLE C. KENTON
Produced by PAUL MALVERN • Executive Producer: JOE GERSHENSON

'HOUSE OF DRACULA' ABLAZE

CREDITS

UNIVERSAL
presents
"HOUSE
OF
DRACULA"
with
Lon Chaney - Martha O'Driscoll
John Carradine - Lionel Atwill
Onslow Stevens - Glenn Strange
Jane Adams - Ludwig Stossel

Original Screenplay
by
Edward T. Lowe

Director of Photography: George
Robinson, A.S.C.; Film Editor: Russell Schoengarth; Art Direction: John
B. Goodman, Martin Obzina; Director of Sound: Bernard B. Brown,
Technician: Jess Moulin; Set Decorations: Russell A. Gausman, Arthur
D. Leddy; Gowns: Vera West; Makeup Artist: Jack P. Pierce; Hair Stylist: Carmen Dirigo; Special Photography by John P. Fulton, A.S.C.;Musical Director: Edgar Fairchild; Assistant Director: Ralph Slosser.

Directed
by
Erle C. Kenton

Produced
by
Paul Malvern

Executive Producer
Joe Gershenson

A UNIVERSAL PICTURE

THE CAST

Talbot . . . . .Lon Chaney
Dracula . . . . .John Carradine
Miliza . . . . .Martha O'Driscoll
Holtz . . . . .Lionel Atwill
Nina . . . . .Jane Adams
Edelman . . . . .Onslow Stevens
Zeigfried . . . . .Ludwig Stossel
Monster . . . . .Glenn Strange
Steinmuhl . . . . .Skelton Knaggs
Brahms . . . . .Joseph E. Bernard
Villager . . . . .Dick Dickinson
Gendarme . . . . .Fred Cordova
Gendarme . . . . .Carey Harrison
Villager . . . . .Harry Lamont
Johannes . . . . .Gregory Muradian
Mother . . . . .Beatrice Gray

SYNOPSIS

(Not for Publication)

Engaged in research to discover a culture to correct human deformities, Dr. Edelman (Onslow Stevens), eminent European scientist, is tricked into aiding the vampire, Count Dracula (John Carradine), who has betrayed an unholy interest in the doctor's attractive assistant, Miliza (Martha O'Driscoll).

Meanwhile, Larry Talbot (Lon Chaney) solicits Edelman's help in relieving a brain pressure which, at the full of the moon, transforms the young man into a werewolf. Not satisfied with the scientist's promise of a future operation to correct the infirmity, Talbot attempts suicide by throwing himself into the Devil's Cave where Edelman discovers the Frankenstein Monster.

Despite the advice of a hunchback, Nina (Jane Adams), whom Edelmann is trying to cure, life is restored to the monster. Edelman's blood, however, has become contaminated following a transfusion with Count Dracula. Beginning to resemble his patient, Edelman performs a successful operation on Talbot, then murders the housekeeper, Ziegfreid (Ludwig Stossel).

The now mad scientist releases the Frankenstein monster which goes berserk carrying Edelman and Nina to their deaths. In the aftermath of the tragedy, Miliza and Talbot, the latter completely cured, are united

Wolf Man, Frankenstein Monster, Dracula United

(Advance)

Three of the screen's most famous and fearsome horror characters, are teamed in Universal's "House of Dracula," due _____ at the _____ Theatre. Lon Chaney appears as the Wolf Man. John Carradine is seen as Count Dracula, human vampire, while Glenn Strange portrays the Frankenstein Monster.

The original screenplay by Edward T. Lowe, described as an outstanding example of shudder-literature, deals with the dubious surgical experiments of a noted European scientist. Onslow Stevens, one of Hollywood's most competent performers, has this unique role. His attempts to remove the werewolf curse from one of his patients gives the story its arresting motivation.

Portrays Vampire

Count Dracula is another of the scientist's subjects and it is the batman's interest in the surgeon's beautiful assistant that brings the plot to its eerie climax. Martha O'Drsicoll has the dramatic role of the assistant. Another popular actress, Jane Adams, appears as a hunchback, who, in the end, is killed by the Frankenstein fiend.

Startling photographic effects by cameraman George Robinson, are said to intensify the film's fascinating qualities.

Directed by Erle C. Kenton, "House of Dracula," is declared to be a worthy successor to Universal's recent "House of Frankenstein" which is rated as one of Hollywood's most colorful box-office sensations.

Paul Malvern was the producer of "House of Dracula." Presiding over the picture's staff was Executive Producer, Joe Gershenson.

HOUSE OF DRACULA (1D)
Martha O'Driscoll and Lon Chaney are teamed romantically in Universal's "House of Dracula."

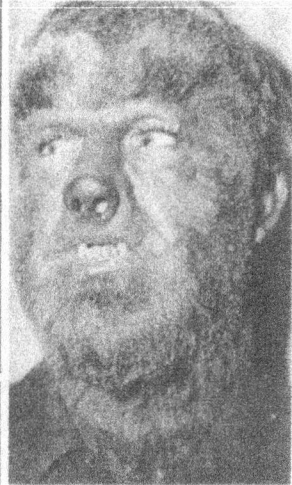
HOUSE OF DRACULA (1E)
Lon Chaney as the Wolf Man in Universal's "House of Dracula."

'House of Dracula' Has Ludwig Stossel

(Advance)

Screen veteran Ludwig Stossel plays an important featured role in Universal's "House of Dracula," which opens _____ at the _____ Theatre. The character thespian is seen as the efficient housekeeper to the psychopathic scientist, played by Onslow Stevens.

The film has Lon Chaney as the Wolf Man, John Carradine as Count Dracula and Glenn Strange as the Frankenstein Monster.

Martha O'Driscoll and Jane Adams play featured feminine roles.

'House of Dracula' Film Based On Eerie Legends

(Current)

Theatregoers inclined to scoff at the Dracula and Wolf Man portrayals in Universal's current "House of Dracula" are not aware that those legends still exist in other parts of the world. The new horror production is now at the _____ Theatre.

The Gypsy peoples of the Balkan States, for instance, still believe that at certain times and under certain conditions a man can become a werewolf.

Under these conditions, the superstitious maintain, actual physical changes take place and the body of the bewitched assumes the character of a beast.

The Dracula or vampire legend is still current in isolated areas of South America. Basis for the belief exists along the Amazon River where giant-sized bats with a wing spread up to three feet fly by night and thrive on the blood of human beings.

Lon Chaney portrays the hideous Wolf Man role in "House of Dracula." During the full of the moon he is transformed into a Wolf Man. Under the influence of the moon he stalks the countryside for human prey.

The Dracula legend is enacted by Shakespearean thespian John Carradine. He is a corpse by day and makes only nocturnal appearances in quest of human blood.

The famous Frankenstein Monster, another sensation of the picture, is impersonated by Glenn Strange. Other performers in "House of Dracula" are Martha O'Driscoll, Lionel Atwill, Onslow Stevens, Jane Adams and Ludwig Stossel.

HOUSE OF DRACULA (2B)
Lovely Martha O'Driscoll faces ghoulish perils in Universal's most terrifying and spine-tingling horror production, "House of Dracula."

Martha O'Driscoll Seen In Uncanny Movie Makeup

(Current)

Martha O'Driscoll's green make-up, appropriately named "Colleen" by the Irish actress, is not likely to launch a fad with Milady.

The spinach colored compound was worn by Martha in her current Universal "House of Dracula" role. The new horror film is now playing at the _____ Theatre.

When filmed in black and white the "Colleen" facial application creates a death pallor to the wearer.

In the horror film, lovely Martha is hypnotized by John Carradine, the latter in the role of a cinema human vampire.

As the actress lingers in the transitional period between life and death her normal complexion assumes a death pallor hue.

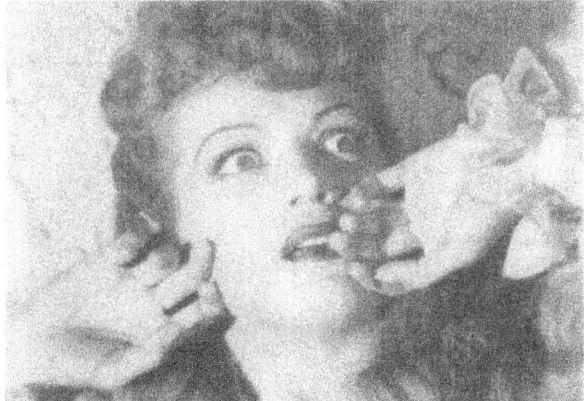
HOUSE OF DRACULA (KB)
Martha O'Driscoll

Shock Movie Boasts Three Film Fiends

(Current)

The Wolf Man, Count Dracula and the Frankenstein Monster form the horror trio in Universal's current screen shocker, "House of Dracula," now playing at the _____ Theatre. The three movie demons are portrayed respectively by Lon Chaney, John Carradine and Glenn Strange.

The shuddery story, dealing with the eerie experiments of a neurotic scientist, revolves around the weird activities of the fiendish threesome. Martha O'Driscoll, Onslow Stevens, Jane Adams and Ludwig Stossel are prominent in the excellent cast.

"House of Dracula," an original screenplay by Edward T. Lowe, was directed by Erle C. Kenton. Paul Malvern was the producer.

DEMONS BRING NEW HORRORS

Spooky Picture Has Emotional Melodic Effect
(Current)

Soft lights and sweet music afford an ideal background for a romantic setting. Universal's "House of Dracula," now at the .... Theatre, has the soft lights but the music is not so sweet.

The horror vehicle's lone musical offering is Beethoven's beautiful "Moonlight Sonata." Martha O'Driscoll performs the master's noted work in true Carnegie Hall manner until - - -

As the action progresses, gaunt John Carradine, in his familiar screen portrayal of Count Dracula, enters and casts a hypnotic spell upon the unsuspecting Martha.

Horror Music

Suddenly the harmony is modulated into a strange, almost discordant minor, a pagan musical distortion which is no longer peaceful or beautiful.

"Goonish characters," claimed Director Erle C. Kenton, "were not enough to carry a picture of this type.

"Proper musical and lighting effects are just as important as the ghoulish creations of the author."

George Robinson, ace Hollywood cameraman, superintended the "Dracula" soft lights department.

All sun arcs and stage lamps, capable of turning night into day, were purposely shaded for every scene in the film.

Lon Chaney portrays the Wolf Man in "House of Dracula." Glenn Strange has the role of the Frankenstein Monster while other prominent players in the cast include Lionel Atwill, Onslow Stevens, Jane Adams and Ludwig Stossel. Paul Malvern was the producer.

HOUSE OF DRACULA (2C)

Martha O'Driscoll and Lon Chaney add romance to the furious action of Universal's horrific and haunting production, "House of Dracula."

Frankenstein Monster Is Everlasting Film Fiend
(Current)

While world savants discuss the future of the "Manhattan Project," otherwise known as the Atomic Bomb, a lone Hollywood script scientist is currently concerned with the future of the "Universal Project" cinematically referred to as the Atomic Anatomy of the Frankenstein Monster.

The problem of permanent detonation has been placed squarely in the lap of Edward T. Lowe, author of Universal's current "House of Dracula," featuring Glenn Strange as the towering Frankenstein monstrosity. The new horror drama is now at the .... Theatre.

A few seasons ago, the studio released Lowe's "House of Frankenstein." That picture was to be the final requiem for the Frankenstein creation. Final footage showed it buried under tons of quicksand.

It was exhuméd, and revived however, following that vehicle's box office success.

Finds Fiend

Lon Chaney, as the Wolf Man, discovers the Monster in the dank Devil's Cave and removes it to the dungeon laboratory of the mad Visarian scientist, played by Onslow Stevens.

Stevens applies an electrical hotfoot to the Monster's neck and it once again becomes a walking booby-trap.

Asserted death is again its reward in the conclusion of "House of Dracula." It is catapulted into a burning cellar following a campaign of carnage and confusion in the castle of its creator.

John Carradine portrays Count Dracula in the weird action of "House of Dracula." Other notables in the large cast include Martha O'Driscoll, Lionel Atwill, Onslow Stevens, Jane Adams and Ludwig Stossel. Erle C. Kenton was the director.

HOUSE OF DRACULA (1A)

Vivacious Martha O'Driscoll appears with such movie demons as the Wolf Man, Dracula and the Frankenstein Monster in Universal's horror-film, "House of Dracula."

Lon Chaney Sensational As Diabolical Wolf Man
(Current)

During the filming of Universal's "House of Dracula," Lon Chaney, in his fourth portrayal as the hideous Wolf Man, worked a total of three days in that grotesque make-up. The sensational new horror drama is now at the .... Theatre.

Chaney, in the film, plays a straight role as Larry Talbot, however, during the full of the moon, Talbot is transformed into a Wolf Man.

The "Werewolf" make-up required six hours to apply and forty-five minutes to remove.

Universal's make-up artist Jack Pierce is the creator of the Wolf Man.

Strange Disguise

Lon's head, face, hands and feet were completely covered with Yak hair. The Yak strands were obtained by the studio from China.

The Yak strands were cut into two inch lengths and applied to the actor's face by liquid rubber. Lon's face had to be completely void of his own hair before the application of Yak hair. Consequently, before the Yak hair was attached to his face, Lon underwent a close barber's shave.

To quote Lon: "the Wolf Man make-up itched like a million red ants, but I didn't dare scratch."

Between scenes he smoked cigarets by using a six inch holder. He drank water through a tube.

During the process of changing from Larry Talbot into the Wolf Man, the actor had to remain immobile for sixteen hours.

Transformation Filmed

The camera, during the transformation period, recorded the eight various stages of the change over from Larry Talbot to the Wolf Man.

This unusual make-up required Chaney to report to the Universal

Make-Up Department at 4 A.M. each morning when he had a 10 o'clock call for his Wolf Man role.

With Chaney in the eerie picture are John Carradine, Martha O'Driscoll, Lionel Atwill, Onslow Stevens, Glenn Strange, Jane Adams and Ludwig Stossel. Erle C. Kenton directed under the producership of Paul Malvern. The Executive Producer was Joe Gershenson.

'House of Dracula' Has John Carradine
(Current)

Long hair John Carradine has gone "Butch!"

The noted Shapespearean actor was shorn of his shoulder length tresses for his Dracula role in Universal's "House of Dracula" now at the .... Theatre.

Carradine's Buffalo Bill hair-do had long been one of Hollywood Boulevard's trade marks.

But the Carradine coiffure was ordered "clipped" by Producer Paul Malvern when the actor signed for his second Universal Dracula portrayal.

Lon Chaney, Martha O'Driscoll, Lionel Atwill, Onslow Stevens, Glenn Strange, Jane Adams and Ludwig Stossel are featured with Carradine in "House of Dracula." Erle C. Kenton directed.

Jane Adams Given Unusual Sobriquet
(Advance)

Toni (The Number) Seven will have to look to her laurels.

A trio of San Quenten Penitentury inmates recently designated Universal's Jane Adams as "The Number."

Judging from the letter received by the petite actress during the making of Universal's "House of Dracula," the title was not bestowed in a numerical sense. Jane has a leading role in the new horror film which comes....... to the .... Theatre.

The big house confinees clearly indicated that "The Number" was significant of It, Sex Appeal and Glamour.

"In other words," the letter read, "you're a number."

The letter concluded with a cryptic P.S. "We're your fans for "life."

Lon Chaney portrays the Wolf Man in "House of Dracula." In the cast are John Carradine, Lionel Atwill, Onslow Stevens, Glenn Strange, Martha O'Drsicoll and Ludwig Stossel. Erle C. Kenton was the director.

HOUSE OF DRACULA (HA)

Jane Adams

Promise Shudders For Thrill Seekers
(Advance)

"House of Dracula," Universal's most recent horror production, comes .... to the .... Theatre. Announced as a successor to the studio's "House of Frankenstein," the new shudder-drama features the three movie demons, the Wolf Man, Count Dracula, human vampire, and the Frankenstein Monster.

Lon Chaney portrays the hideous Wolf Man. John Carradine is seen as Count Dracula and Glenn Strange appears as the fearsome Frankenstein Manster.

Martha O'Driscoll, Lionel Atwill, Onslow Stevens, Jane Adams and Ludwig Stossel are other competent players in the supporting cast. Erle C. Kenton directed from the original screenplay by Edward T. Lowe. Paul Malvern was the producer.

HOUSE OF DRACULA (1F)

John Carradine appears as Count Dracula, human vampire, in Universal's latest and creepiest horror production, "House of Dracula."

CHILLFILM HAS MONSTER TRIO

HOUSE OF DRACULA (2A)

"House of Dracula," Universal's devastating new horror film, has Lon Chaney as the Wolf Man, John Carradine as Count Dracula, and Glenn Strange in the role of the eerie and ferocious Frankenstein Monster.

Weird Screen Effect in Bizarre Film Drama Told
(Advance)

Keep your eyes on the monsters and you won't catch a technical fault in Universal's "House of Dracula" which comes .... to the .... Theatre.

Reveal Odd Twists In Cinema Careers
(Current)

Hollywood would have been minus three top performing horror characters if early ambitions had been realized by John Carradine, Lon Chaney and Glenn Strange.

The magic lure of grease paint prevented Carradine from donning judicial robes and ascending the Supreme Court Bench. Lon turned his back on his intended career as a public utility tycoon and chose to follow the footsteps of his late father. If young Glenn Strange had listened to his mother's advice he would be a practicing minister in Texas.

Today the trio is appearing in Universal's "House of Dracula," as Count Dracula, the Wolf Man and the Frankenstein Monster, respectively. The eerie movie shocker, now at the .... Theatre, is a worthy successor to Universal's recent "House of Frankenstein."

Seen in the supporting cast of the new production are Martha O'Driscoll, Lionel Atwill, Onslow Stevens, Jane Adams and Ludwig Stossel.

Hometowns, Birthdates of Players

Lon Chaney	Oklahoma City, Okla.	Feb. 10
Martha O'Driscoll	Tulsa, Okla.	March 4
John Carradine	New York City, N. Y.	Feb. 5
Lionel Atwill	Croydon, England	March 1
Onslow Stevens	Los Angeles, Calif.	March 29
Glenn Strange	Carlsbad, New Mexico	Aug. 16
Jane Adams	San Antonio, Tex.	Aug. 7

Stark Drama Enacted in Lurid 'House of Dracula'
(Review)

Arm yourself with an anti-goose pimple lotion! Universal's "House of Dracula" has moved into the .... Theatre. The horror vehicle, a successor to that studio's recent "House of Frankenstein," reunites the terror threesome, Lon Chaney as the Wolf Man, John Carradine as Count Dracula, the human vampire; and Glenn Strange in the role of the Frankenstein Monster.

In addition, there is a fiendish* scientist played by character actor Onslow Stevens. Glamorous Martha O'Driscoll has a leading role and Jane Adams, former Conover beauty, is cast in the grotesque role of the hunchback assistant to the sinister scientist.

Edward T. Lowe's original screen story concerns the exploits of the scientist in attempting to administer medical aid to the maladjusted monster trio.

Lon Chaney turns in his fourth convincing portrayal as Larry Talbot the Wolf Man.

Dependable Demons

Shakespearean actor John Carradine and Glenn Strange lend able assistance to the Universal terror thespian as the cadaverous Count Dracula and the Frankenstein Monster, respectively.

Lovely Miss O'Driscoll injects a romantic theme into the horror offering in her role as the laboratory aide to the mad physician. Out of pity for the plight of Lon Chaney, who is transformed into a Wolf Man at the full of the moon, Martha falls in love with the otherwise personable but unfortunate young man.

Supporting roles are masterfully handled by Lionel Atwill as inspector Holtz and Ludwig Stossel as housekeeper to the frenzied physician.

The film was produced by Paul Malvern. Erle E. Kenton's direction is outstanding as is the effective photography by George Robinson. The Executive Producer was Joe Gershenson.

Need Yak Hair For Movie Thrill
(Current)

An acute Yak hair shortage has struck Universal Studio's make-up department.

The Yak, or bovine raminant, an inhabitant of the higher regions of central Asia, has been the sole provider of hair which constitutes the major portion of Lon Chaney's make-up for his weird Wolf Man roles.

It was learned recently that the studio's make-up department had just enough Yak strands left to transform the character actor into his Wolf Man attire for the current "House of Dracula." The new scare film is now at the .... Theatre.

The studio received its last Yak hair shipment from the Orient prior to the war. Three "Wolf Man" features have been filmed since then.

Other "horror" characters in "House of Dracula" are Count Dracula, played by John Carradine, and the Frankenstein Monster, impersonated by Glenn Strange. Erle C. Kenton directed.

The picture's opening (column 2)

At the picture's opening a huge bat approaches the open bedroom of Martha O'Driscoll.

The bat remains motionless-his eyes fixed on the slumbering figure of Miss O'Driscoll.

Slowly before the eyes of the awed audience a transformation takes place. The bat disappears and in its place emerges John Carradine as Count Dracula.

Carradine enters the open window, passes by a tiny dresser and pauses beside the bed of Martha.

Portrait of Actress

On the dresser, now in the background, is a tiny framed portrait. The outline of the person is not distinguishable—but it's Martha O'Driscoll.

Why that photo represents a technical fault is simply because the bedroom scenes take place in 1881 and the portrait is a head shot of Martha taken from her first motion picture, "Collegiate," filmed in 1935.

The "good luck" portrait has been with Martha in each subsequent picture.

Lon Chaney gives his famous Wolf Man portrayal in "House of Dracula." Others in the impressive cast are Lionel Atwill, Onslow Stevens, Glenn Strange, Jane Adams and Ludwig Strossel. Erle C. Kenton directed.

HOUSE OF DRACULA (1C)

Beautiful Jane Adams has an outstanding dramatic role in Universal's exciting "House of Dracula."

Lionel Atwill Seen In Horror Picture
(Advance)

Lionel Atwill, famed for his Nazi portrayals, is featured as a police inspector in Universal's "House of Dracula," which opens .... at the .... Theatre.

The super-horror vehicle, successor to "House of Frankenstein," reunites Lon Chaney, as the Wolf Man, John Carradine in his familiar Count Dracula role and Glenn Strange as the Frankenstein Monster.

Feminine honors are shared by Martha O'Driscoll and Jane Adams. The film was directed by Erle C. Kenton and produced by Paul Malvern.

PRODUCTION HIGHLIGHTS

Lon Chaney's make-up as the Wolf Man in Universal's "House of Dracula" required six hours to apply.

Jane Adams, cast as a hunchback in Universal's "House of Dracula," was a former Conover model.

Universal's current "House of Dracula" is a companion picture to "House of Frankenstein," which was released by that studio several seasons ago and proved one of the company's biggest grossers.

Jane Adams, discovered by Walter Wanger as a "Salome" girl, receives her first dramatic role in Universal's "House of Dracula."

Paul Malvern, producer of Universal's "House of Dracula," was a former member of an acrobatic troupe.

The Frankenstein Monster makes his seventh cinematic appearance in Universal's "House of Dracula." Role was created by Boris Karloff and is portrayed by Glenn Strange in the current horror film.

Although Lon Chaney's Wolf Man make-up in Universal's "House of Dracula" is ghoulish to behold—it is not injurious!

Although Lon Chaney's face is completely covered with Yak hair for his Wolf Man portrayal in "House of Dracula," the actor's face had to be clean shaven before the bovine strands were attached with rubber cement.

Lovely Irish actress Martha O'Driscoll wears a green make-up compound in "House of Dracula." The horror vehicle is filmed in black and white—but the spinach colored application was required to create a death pallor when the actress was hypnotized by John Carradine portraying the human vampire.

HOUSE OF DRACULA (1B)

The Frankenstein Monster, frightening demon of the screen's major horror films, is portrayed by Glenn Strange in Universal's latest chill-drama, "House of Dracula."

FREE RECORDINGS

MR. SHOWMAN . . . Have you been taking advantage of the wonderful opportunity radio offers you for selling your presentation? If you haven't been telling 'em about it on the air, it's time you made use of Universal's timely transcription service to exhibitors all over the country. Knowing the showman's problems and realizing the need for radio copy with plenty of selling punch, we've prepared a socko transcription on "HOUSE OF DRACULA."

There are six station breaks of ten seconds each, two full minute announcements, and two half-minute spots. Ample time has been provided to accommodate "live" announcements of your playdates and theatre name. Get your discs NOW . . . THEY ARE FREE!

Write, Wire or Phone to the
EXPLOITATION DEPARTMENT
Universal Studio, Universal City, Calif.

START DISCUSSIONS

The scientific background of "HOUSE OF DRA-CULA" can get you plenty of printer's ink to stir up talk about the film, if you can get local scientists or doctors to publicly express their ideas as to whether or not a man-made monster can be brought back to life after many years of sleep.

Modern science has actually created life, and has kept human organs, which have been separated from the body, alive as was proved by the much publicized beating heart in the famous machine created by Dr. Alexis Carrel and Charles A. Lindbergh.

Play up this angle by tying in with the newspapers for a series of interviews with local scientists on whether the situations which occur in "HOUSE OF DRACULA" are possible.

CHEMICAL DISPLAY

Several sequences in the film suggest a chemical paraphernalia display which you can set up in your lobby a week or so in advance of the picture's opening. It will help put over the weird, scientific angle of the "HOUSE OF DRACULA" and will get them talking.

Tie-up with a local drug or chemical house and promote an assortment of beakers, bottles and other similar apparatus such as test tubes and retorts. Fill glass vessels with different colored water and in some of the retorts you can employ the use of dry ice to give off a weird and impressive boiling effect. Perhaps your house electrician can rig up a phoney instrument panel with a spark gap arrangement which will give the whole display an authentic aspect.

Use a card with copy as follows . . . *SEE HOW MAN'S SCIENTIFIC GENIUS CONTROLS THE WORLD'S MOST AMAZING CHARACTERS . . .! IT'S THE YEAR'S MOST THRILLING ADVENTURE "HOUSE OF DRACULA" NEXT WEEK!!*

SHADOWGRAPH

The sketch suggests an advance display for your inner lobby. Rig up a small spot with flasher attachment just inside and over the entrance door. In front of this hang a small cut out figure of Dracula with cape spread (like bat wings). The shadow will be cast on the wall ahead. On a separate spotlight (also with flasher) have stencil cut to throw wording: "Coming events cast their shadows . . . in the 'House of Dracula'." The effect will be message and shadow of Dracula will alternate on wall and sometimes both will show together. This is a good attraction getter to attract customers for your opening.

ORDER YOUR HORROR TRAILER EARLY
FROM
NATIONAL SCREEN SERVICE

BUILD AN ANIMATED LOBBY DISPLAY

This is an animated lobby display which is made from life-size blow-ups of three of the principal characters in the film . . . The sinister DRA-CULA . . . The weird MONSTER . . . and the WOLFMAN!! These stills are in your exchange set numbers 5 . . . 27 . . . and 73.

Remove the out-stretched arms from the Dracula figure and re-assemble them with a nut and bolt arrangement so that they move freely to the out-stretched position and then back down to the sides of the body. This movement can be accomplished by a small electric motor which your house electrician can regulate to the desired speed. Be careful that the arms do not move too fast because a fast jerky motion will spoil the effect.

Now get a large flowing cape similar to the one worn by John Carradine as Dracula. It should be one of the full opera capes with plenty of folds. This is draped over the arms of the figure to give it a life-like appearance.

Cut out the heads of the Wolfman and the Monster and mount them behind the figure of Dracula so that they are hidden by the caps when the arms are out-stretched. When the arms come down to the sides of the body the two cutout heads are revealed.

It would probably be more effective if the three figures used in this display were blown up a little larger than life-size, to make the entire display more impressive.

Copy should be along these lines . . . *THE MIGHTIEST MONSTERS OF ALL TIME . . . IN THE YEAR'S GREATEST EPIC OF UNBELIEVABLE THRILLS! "HOUSE OF DRACULA" STARTS FRIDAY!!*

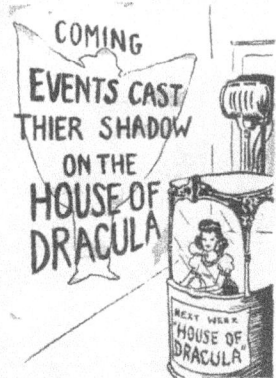

GIVE HORROR TREATMENT TO LOBBY

Every smart showman knows the value of his front and lobby on a horror picture. In "HOUSE OF DRACULA" you have a natural for this type of ballyhoo . . . give it everything in the book!

By the use of sectional compoboard flats masked over the front of your theatre you can create the "House of Dracula." On each side of the entrance build the windows with tumble-down shutters. For these follow the idea of the silhouette display described and shown below. If your box-office is in center of lobby it should also be covered with a panel of the house and provide a practical window through which ticket seller can transact business. Arrange heads of Dracula, the Mad Doctor, the Wolf Man and the Frankenstein Monster across the openings as shown. Inside the lobby against the side walls arrange cut-outs of Dracula and the other horror characters. Flying bats suspended on strings, black cats, cobwebs, etc., will complete the effect. All lighting should be in green and red with shadow effects to create an eerie atmosphere. Sound effect screams and weird noises will add to the illusion.

SHADOW DISPLAY

SEE THE GREATEST COLLECTION OF HORROR CHARACTERS EVER GATHERED TOGETHER FOR ONE PICTURE, ALL IN . . . . HOUSE OF DRACULA

Have your artist fix up a series of silhouette displays, along the lines suggested in the sketch for your lobby walls. Make them of painted compoboard with the window glass cut out and covered with a transparency. Cut-out figures placed between the transparency and a light will produce shadows on the window. For a moving horror display have one figure with knife in hand move back and forth by means of a slow turning motor. Copy should read . . . "HORRORS . . . CHILLS . . . TERRORS . . . ALL ABIDE IN THE 'HOUSE OF DRACULA'."

LUMINOUS POSTERS

Here's an effective way to make your one sheet posters more attractive. Go over the title, and large heads with a good grade of phosphorescent paint and spot them in a dark corner of your inside lobby a week or so in advance of playdate. To punch them out, light with a green or violet baby spot, and arrange for a flasher to have them go on and off intermittently.

'HOUSE' IN LOBBY

Here's an exploitation idea that should cause a lot of comment around town, and at the same time provide plenty of material for newspaper copy.

Devote one wall of your lobby, or a corner if it is more suitable, to a replica of a typical haunted house. You can build it out of compo-board, wood and cardboard. A few boards missing here and there, a broken window pane, several shutters hanging loosely, and perhaps phony cob webs will give the impression of weirdness and will get over the atmosphere that you want.

Build up word of mouth interest by inserting several small ads in the papers. Use a teaser type ad with the following copy: . . . *HAVE YOU SEEN THE STRANGE "HOUSE OF DRACULA" IN THE LOBBY OF THE RIVOLI THEATRE? THERE'LL BE SOME WEIRD THINGS HAPPENING THERE ON THE NIGHT OF (GIVE DATE WHICH CAN BE THE NIGHT BEFORE YOU OPEN THE PICTURE) . . . BE THERE IF YOU CAN STAND THE SHOCK!* Promote a few news stories if possible.

With the expert assistance of your house electrician and sound man you can work out all sorts of scarey and weird stunts. Mount cut-outs of some of the main characters in the windows of the house with spots focused on them. Electrician can arrange to have the lights go on and off at various intervals. Strange sounds can emanate from the house, such as piercing screams, gunshots, doors slamming, the clanging of chains, spark gap noises, and other weird effects. A public address system should be set up to provide plenty of volume for a booming voice which mentions HOUSE OF DRACULA in a sinister tone, all through the proceedings.

Rig up several weird figures on a wire so that they can be made to "float" in and out of the house. As you prepare for the stunt other ideas will suggest themselves. Important thing is to let them know about it.

WANT AD TEASER

Insert teaser ads in Classified Ad Columns under "For Rent" and "For Sale." Copy should read as follows: "The 'House of Dracula' is now open for inspection. Terms reasonable. For details see manager of Rivoli Theatre this week." Cover all papers during week of run.

MAGAZINE STANDS

Mystery and horror stories, both in book and pulp magazine form, have become increasingly popular during recent years. Don't pass up the opportunity to capitalize on this ready-made audience. Tie-up with all book stores and magazine stands. As the benefit works both ways, showman should have no trouble getting window cards, stills and counter displays, with permission to stuff magazines with the picture's excellent herald.

For window and counter cards use copy along these lines . . . *OUR COMPLETE STOCK OF MYSTERY AND HORROR BOOKS WILL GIVE YOU PLENTY OF READING THRILLS . . . FOR NEW MOTION PICTURE THRILLS SEE "HOUSE OF DRACULA" AT THE RIVOLI.*

TRIED AND TRUE

This time-honored stunt of a "First Aid for Shock" booth should be taken from your files and dusted off for this picture. Have a white garbed "nurse" in attendance at all times. Build a board to hold the following items: *Cotton Pads . . . "to keep knees from knocking." False Teeth . . . "For those who swallow their own in the excitement." Chewing Gum . . . "to keep teeth from chattering." Wool Socks . . . "in case of cold feet." Safety Belt . . . "to keep you in your chair." Electric Heating Pad . . . "for cold shivers." Smelling Salts . . . "in case of severe shock." Hair Dye . . . "for those whose hair turns white." Hospital Phone Number . . . "in case of emergency."*

The "nurse" could also give out envelopes containing several ordinary candy "red-drops," which look like pills. Copy should read: "To steady your nerves during the picture take one every five minutes."

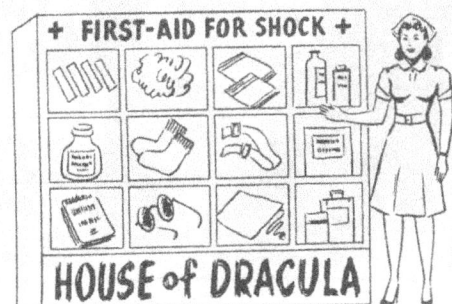

DRACULA
FRANKENSTEIN'S
MONSTER
WOLF MAN
MAD DOCTOR
HUNCHBACK

HOUSE
OF
DRACULA

with Lon CHANEY · Martha O'DRISCOLL
John CARRADINE · Lionel ATWILL
Onslow Stevens · Glenn Strange
Jane Adams · Ludwig Stossel

A UNIVERSAL PICTURE 104

Ad No. 104—1 Col. Mat

DRACULA
FRANKENSTEIN'S MONSTER
WOLF MAN
MAD DOCTOR
HUNCHBACK

HOUSE OF
DRACULA

with Lon CHANEY · Martha O'DRISCOLL
John CARRADINE · Lionel ATWILL
Onslow Stevens · Glenn Strange
Jane Adams · Ludwig Stossel

A UNIVERSAL PICTURE 103

Ad No. 103—1 Col. Mat

FRANKENSTEIN'S
MONSTER

DRACULA

WOLF MAN

MAD DOCTOR

HUNCHBACK

IT'S MONSTER-RIFIC!
The screen's ALL NEW
super-shock sensation!

HOUSE
OF
DRACULA

UNIVERSAL'S spectacular sequel to
"House of Frankenstein"

with
Lon CHANEY · Martha O'DRISCOLL
John CARRADINE · Lionel ATWILL
ONSLOW STEVENS · GLENN STRANGE
JANE ADAMS · LUDWIG STOSSEL

Original Screenplay by Edward T. Lowe · Directed by ERLE C. KENTON
Produced by PAUL MALVERN · Executive Producer: JOE GERSHENSON

207

Ad No. 207—2 Col. Mat

DRACULA
FRANKENSTEIN'S
MONSTER
WOLF MAN
MAD DOCTOR
HUNCHBACK

The Mightiest Monsters of All Time!
Universal Presents

HOUSE OF
DRACULA

LON CHANEY   MARTHA O'DRISCOLL
JOHN CARRADINE   LIONEL ATWILL
Onslow Stevens   Glenn Strange   Jane Adams   Ludwig Stossel

202

Ad No. 202—2 Col. Mat

UNIVERSAL PRESENTS

DRACULA!
FRANKENSTEIN'S
MONSTER!
WOLF MAN!
MAD DOCTOR!
HUNCHBACK!

HOUSE OF DRACULA

with
LON CHANEY   MARTHA O'DRISCOLL
JOHN CARRADINE   LIONEL ATWILL
Onslow Stevens   Glenn Strange   Jane Adams   Ludwig Stossel

105

Ad No. 105—1 Col. Mat

ALL TOGETHER! All NEW Sensations!

Universal Presents

HOUSE OF DRACULA

DRACULA!
FRANKENSTEIN'S
MONSTER!
WOLF MAN!
MAD DOCTOR!
HUNCHBACK!

with
LON CHANEY   MARTHA O'DRISCOLL
JOHN CARRADINE   LIONEL ATWILL
Onslow Stevens   Glenn Strange   Jane Adams   Ludwig Stossel

Original Screenplay by Edward T. Lowe · Directed by ERLE C. KENTON
Produced by PAUL MALVERN · Executive Producer: JOE GERSHENSON

205

Ad No. 205—2 Col. Mat

ALL NEW!
ALL TOGETHER!
The Mightiest Monsters
of All Time!

DRACULA

FRANKENSTEIN'S MONSTER

WOLF MAN

MAD DOCTOR

HUNCHBACK

HOUSE OF DRACULA

UNIVERSAL'S
Spectacular Sequel to
"House of Frankenstein"

with
LON CHANEY · MARTHA O'DRISCOLL
JOHN CARRADINE · LIONEL ATWILL
ONSLOW STEVENS · GLENN STRANGE
JANE ADAMS · LUDWIG STOSSEL
Original Screenplay by Edward T. Lowe · Directed by ERLE C. KENTON
Produced by PAUL MALVERN · Executive Producer: JOE GERSHENSON

208

Ad No. 208—2 Col. Mat

Ad No. 106—1 Col. Mat

ALL TOGETHER! ALL NEW SENSATIONS!

FRANKENSTEIN'S MONSTER

DRACULA

WOLF MAN

MAD DOCTOR

HUNCHBACK

The Mightiest of all Screen Monsters!

HOUSE OF DRACULA

Universal's Spectacular Sequel to "House of Frankenstein"!

with

LON CHANEY · MARTHA O'DRISCOLL
JOHN CARRADINE · LIONEL ATWILL
ONSLOW STEVENS · GLENN STRANGE
JANE ADAMS · LUDWIG STOSSEL

Original Screenplay by Edward T. Lowe · Directed by ERLE C. KENTON
Produced by PAUL MALVERN · Executive Producer: JOE GERSHENSON

301

Ad No. 301—3 Col. Mat

DRACULA
FRANKENSTEIN'S MONSTER
WOLF MAN
MAD DOCTOR
HUNCHBACK

ALL TOGETHER!
HOUSE OF DRACULA

with LON CHANEY
MARTHA O'DRISCOLL
JOHN CARRADINE
LIONEL ATWILL
Onslow Stevens
Glenn Strange
Jane Adams

201

Ad No. 201—2 Col. Mat

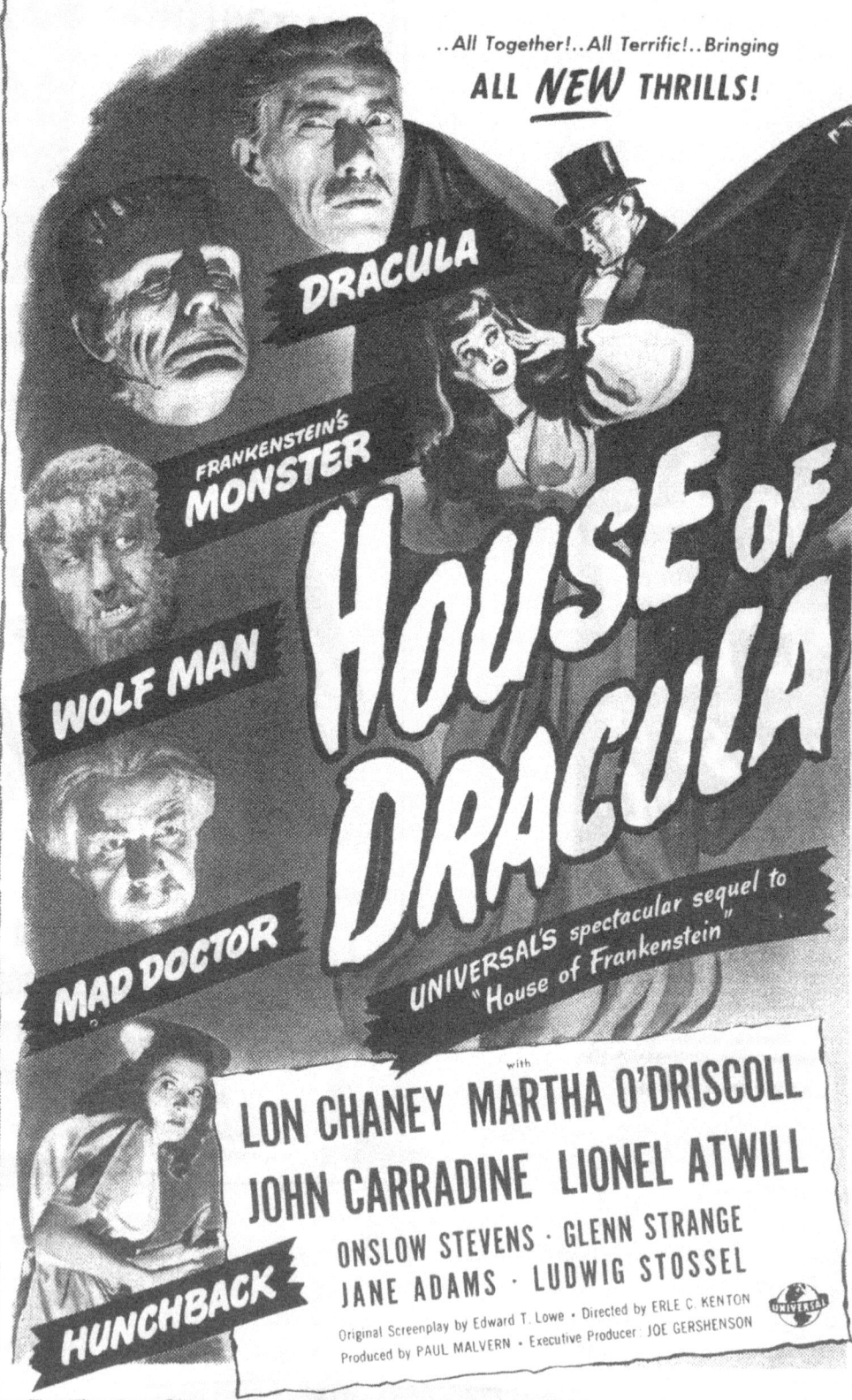

303

ALL TOGETHER! ALL NEW SENSATIONS!

The Mightiest of all Screen Monsters!

FRANKENSTEIN'S MONSTER

DRACULA

WOLF MAN

MAD DOCTOR

HUNCHBACK

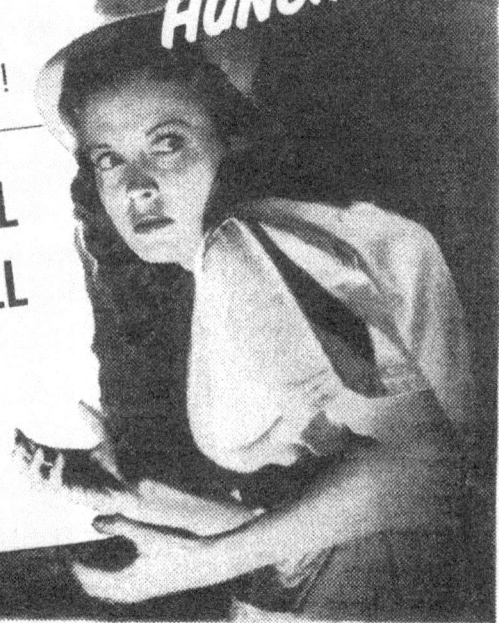

HOUSE of DRACULA

Universal's Spectacular Sequel to "House of Frankenstein"!

with

LON CHANEY · MARTHA O'DRISCOLL
JOHN CARRADINE · LIONEL ATWILL

ONSLOW STEVENS · GLENN STRANGE

JANE ADAMS · LUDWIG STOSSEL

Original Screenplay by Edward T. Lowe · Directed by ERLE C. KENTON
Produced by PAUL MALVERN · Executive Producer: JOE GERSHENSON

401

ALL TOGETHER! All **NEW** Sensations!

The mightiest of all Screen Monsters!

DRACULA! FRANKENSTEIN'S MONSTER! WOLF MAN! MAD DOCTOR! HUNCHBACK!

HOUSE OF DRACULA

Universal's Spectacular Sequel to "House of Frankenstein"!

UNIVERSAL

with Lon **CHANEY** Martha **O'DRISCOLL** John **CARRADINE** Lionel **ATWILL**

ONSLOW STEVENS **GLENN STRANGE** **JANE ADAMS** **LUDWIG STOSSEL**

Original Screenplay by Edward T. Lowe · Directed by ERLE C. KENTON · Produced by PAUL MALVERN · Executive Producer: JOE GERSHENSON

501

Ad No. 501—5 Col. Mat

SPECIAL ADVERTISING STILLS

Five 8x10 Photos of the Key Art used in this Pressbook ad campaign. Excellent material for making Lobbies, Blow-ups and special ads. Available at your National Screen Service Branch.

Glenn Strange's publicity pose is probably the most well known image of the Frankenstein monster for children today. The outstretched arms, large hands and height overshadow the horrid living corpse created by Boris Karloff in Jack Pierce's makeup.

Editor's note: Since *House of Dracula* is not yet available on MCA/Universal Home Video, we present this synopsis (In narrative)

HOUSE OF DRACULA
By
Gregory Wm. Mank
(Based on the 1945 Universal Film)

In her bedroom in the old castle on the craggy seacoast of Visaria, blonde Miliza Morelle is tossing with strange, perverse dreams. Outside her French windows, a large black bat hovers in the night, and, in a strange flurry, is transformed into a tall skeletal man in flowing cape and top hat, who gazes lustfully at Miliza...

Downstairs, the stranger enters the study of Dr. Franz Edelmann, the brilliant scientist renowned for his near-miraculous cures of supposedly hopeless cases. As his cat squeals at the sight of the tall visitor, Edelmann awakes, The stranger introduces himself as Baron Latos and asks Edelmann to escort him to the gloomy old armor room of the castle where the scientist sees a large coffin with the infamous talisman.

"The Dracula crest!" exclaims Dr. Edelmann.

"Yes, doctor, I am Count Dracula. You see before you a man who's lived for centuries, kept alive by the blood of innocent people, That's why I've come to you to seek release from a curse of misery and horror, against which I'm powerless to fight alone. You could effect a cure?''

"It would be a challenge to medical science," muses Edelmann.

"Accept that challenge, doctor, but decide quickly.'' says Dracula, looking toward the great window. The dawn . . .

Edelmann agrees to treat Dracula, unaware that the vampire's true goal lies in the bedroom above, still plagued by nightmares.

The next day Edelmann begins work on developing an antitoxin for Dracula's blood. Assisting him is Nina, a lovely nurse afflicted with a hunched back. Edelmann plans to reward Nina's dedication to his experiments by repairing her deformity via a bone-softening extract culled from an exotic plant known as the Clavaria Formosa, grown in the doctor's laboratory under tropical conditions. Meanwhile that evening, Dracula arrives for a consultation with Edelmann, and sees the doctor's other assistant, Miliza.

"Baron Latos!" smiles the surprised woman.

"Miss Morelle! You left Schoenheim just as we were becoming acquainted. Now that 'chance' has brought us together again, I hope to see you quite often . . . ?"

Edelmann gives Dracula his diagnosis. An examination of his blood has revealed the presence of a hitherto unknown parasite. The scientist hopes that a pure culture of the parasite injected into Dracula's bloodstream, will destroy itself. And Dracula agrees to his first transfusion.

The moon had not yet risen that night when a drawn

stranger arrives at the castle begging for an immediate audience with Edelmann. "If you'll just give him my name . . .Talbot, Lawrence Talbot. . .then he'll understand." Miliza promises that the scientist will see him as soon as the transfusion is over, "There isn't time," raves Talbot, and he races into the night.

Later that evening, the telephone rings at the castle. It proves to be Inspector Holtz asking the doctor to come at once to the town in regard to a stranger in the jail. As Edelmann and Miliza arrive, they see a crowd milling about the station with Steinmuhl, the ugly village idiot, in the fore.

"If I find the person who started the rumor we have a crazy man here," barks Holtz at the mob, "I'll lock him up!"

"As a matter of fact, doctor, we have!" admits Holtz to Edelmann in the privacy of the jailhouse.

"He came here a little while ago and demanded that I put him in a cell to keep him from committing murder! Decent sort of chap otherwise, name of Talbot."

"Doctor," pleads Talbot through the cell bars, "have you ever heard of the pentagram, the mark of the beast? When the full moon rises, I turn into a werewolf, with only one desire in my mind, to kill!"

As Edelmann tries to convince Talbot that his lycnathropy is only in his mind, the prisoner suddenly peers into the moonlight filtering through his cell window. Suddenly, as Edelmann, Holtz and Miliza watch in horror, Talbot gasps and snarls as his face and hands metamorphose into those of a terrible beast, one that leaps at the cell bars, lunging and stretching his claws at the trio of onlookers.

The next morning, Holtz brings Talbot to the castle. "Do you think he can help me?" the lycanthrope asks Miliza, who feels a strange sympathy and attraction toward the haunted Talbot. "He's done some wonderful things," encourages the nurse, and Edelmann offers his diagnosis. He has found, he says, pressure upon certain parts of Talbot's brain which, along with Talbot's belief in his lycanthropy, brings about just that change when the moon is full.

"During the period in which your reasoning processes gives way to self-hypnosis, the glands which govern your metabolism get out of control like a steam engine without a balance wheel. When this happens, the glands generate an abnormal supply of certain hormones, which," implies the doctor, "are responsible for the physical transformation."

Edelmann fears the risk of a surgical operation to enlarge the cranial cavity, but there may be an alternative. In the laboratory, the scientist shows Talbot the Clavaria Formosa plant from which he can extract a substance that can soften any hard substance composed of calcium phosphate, such as the skull. Edelmann hopes to enlarge Talbot's cranial cavity to relieve the pressure.

"You can do that now?" asks Talbot, who receives a sad pause in response, "Can you?"

Edelmann admits he cannot, "It will take some time to produce the mold in sufficient quantities," and he suggests that Talbot confine himself again that night when the moon will be full again.

"No, doctor. No. I can't go through that again!" Talbot races from the castle and to the cliffs above the sea. For a moment he stares at the raging waters far below, then hurls himself into the sea.

That night, in the moonlight, the villagers gather on the cliffs erecting a crane for Edelmann, by which he might lower himself to the rocky shoreline and the Devil's Cave far below, where he hopes the sea has washed Talbot. The scientist meticulously times his actions to the last minute; if he arrives after Talbot changes back into human form, he fears the man will try to kill himself again; if he arrives too early, while Talbot is still a beast, he fears for his own life.

Edelmann ventures into the darkness of the cave. Suddenly a wild snarl sounds and the Wolf Man wrestles the scientist to the cave floor. Seconds before the creatures rips into Edelmann's throat, the moon sets and the beast changes back into a man.

Edelmann tells the despairing Talbot that even though he sought death, he will live because "God in His divine workings, has led you to the very thing which makes help possible." The temperature and humidity in the cave were ideal for growing the spore-producing plants needed for Talbot's cure. Before the next full moon, there should be enough for the process.

Exploring farther into the cavern, the men soon make a startling discovery, There in the mud, is the Frankenstein Monster, cradling the skeleton of Dr. Niemann (Boris

Karloff) whom he had carried into the quicksand years before. "He's still alive!" Talbot exclaims of his old enemy. "He's indestructible," replies Edelmann. "Frankenstein's creation is man's challenge to the laws of life and death!" Talbot calls to the Doctor. He had found and exit in the cave wall. The Castle's recorded history had mentioned an old torture chamber in the lower levels with an entrance to the castle proper, an ideal place for a new laboratory to produce the Clavaria Formosa.

Fascinated by the Monster, Edelmann exhumes him from the mud and brings the comatose creature to the castle laboratory, determined to revive him. Talbot and Nina protest. "Think what you're doing, doctor!" says Nina, "To bring him back again . . .would unleash worse than murder upon humanity . . . Man's responsibility is to his fellow man!" These words convince Edelmann, and he turns off the electrical machinery. "Frankenstein's Monster must never wreak havoc again," says the scientist.

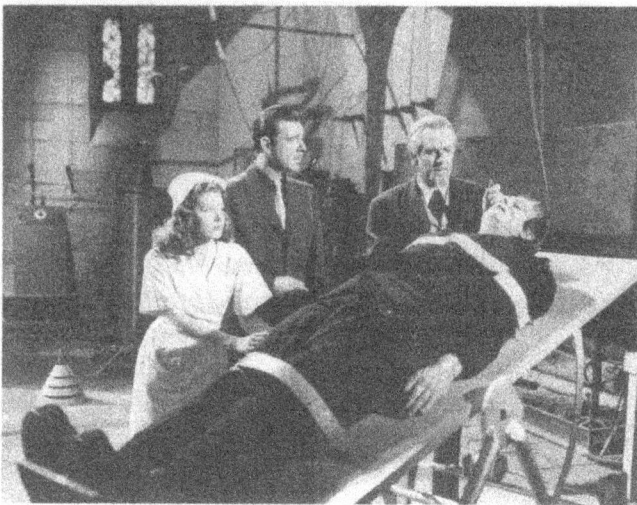

Night falls, and Miliza, in the great hall, is playing "Moonlight Sonata" on the piano as the Count enters. As he gazes at her, suddenly the music changes to a wild, demonic tune. "I've never heard this music before, yet I'm playing it!"

"You're creating it for me!" replies Dracula.

"It frightens me!" replies Miliza.

"It's beautiful! It's the music of the world from which I come." responds Dracula.

"It makes me see strange things; people who are dead yet they're alive. . . .?"

Dracula advances on Miliza, but before he can caress her, a strange impulse causes her to lift a little necklace crucifix from her bodice. Dracula whirls away and the music returns to the "Moonlight Sonata."

Nevertheless, Dracula hovers about the castle that night. When Nina returns from the new laboratory in the cave, she sees Miliza in a passionate trance, standing next to him before a mirror.

"I couldn't see his reflection!" gasps Nina to Edelmann, who rushes into action. He tells her that if anything happens to him, that she is to go to the old armor room in the basement and burn what she finds there.

Outside in the garden, Dracula has succeeded in persuading Miliza to drop her cross. Edelmann appears and coolly asks Dracula back into the castle for another transfusion.

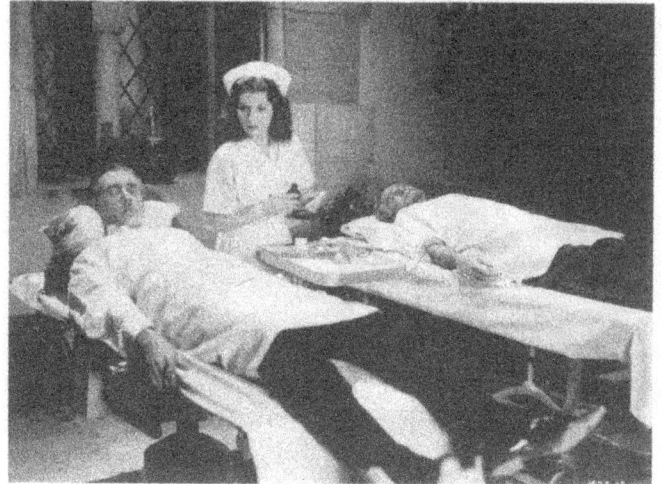

Dracula suavely agrees, but as the scientist loses consciousness during the process, the vampire rises from the operating table, takes the needle of parasite blood and

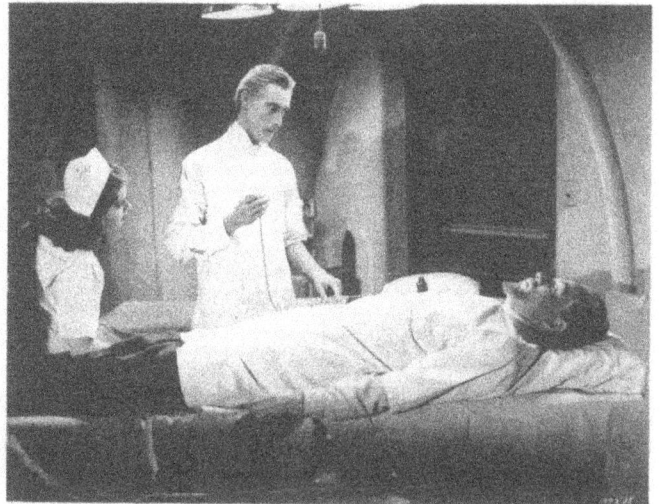

shoots it into Edelmann's bloodstream.

Transformed into a bat, Dracula flies into the bedroom where Miliza, in a negligee, with her hair down, awaits her undead bridegroom. Nina runs to Talbot's room for help and Talbot breaks into Miliza's room, just as Edelmann lunges through another door, waving a cross at the vampire. Dracula races to the armor room to the sanctuary of his coffin, and Edelmann follows. The Doctor drags the coffin into the light of the dawn which reduces Dracula to a skeleton. At the same time, Miliza suddenly breaks from her trance and looks warmly at Talbot.

Not long afterwards, Edelmann begins to feel the presence of Dracula's blood in his veins. Late one evening, as his cat runs in terror, Edelmann watches his reflection in the mirror become hideous and degenerate and then vanish. He collapses into a wild, perverse dream, one in which Dracula rises form the dead, and the Monster rampages through the village and Nina, no longer deformed, now seductively beautiful, walks to him. . .

Awakening, Edelmann runs to the laboratory and begins recharging the Monster, However, the spell passes and the doctor confesses his illness to Nina. He wants to operate on her immediately, but the nurse unselfishly insists that Edelmann operate on Talbot instead, The next

day, Edelmann enlarges Talbots cranial cavity, and orders his nurses to devote all their energies to extracting enough spores for him to perform his operation on Nina as soon as possible. Talbot waits until the next full moon appears, his fears soothed by Miliza. She tells the man with whom she is falling love that he will soon see the night as a time of peace and beauty.

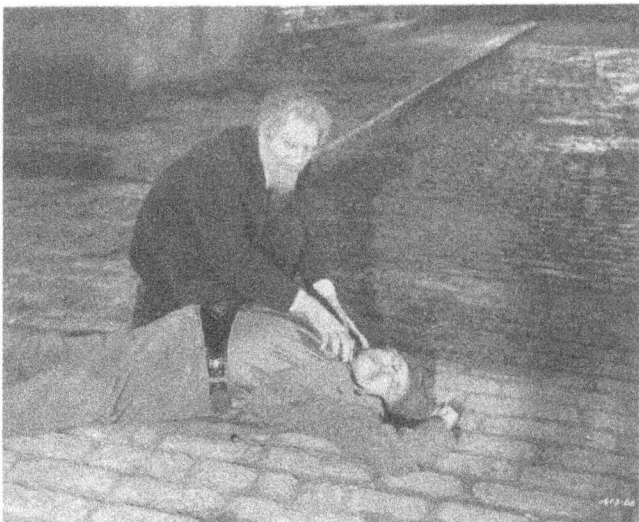

"Until that time comes," answers Talbot, "I'll live a thousand hopes and die a thousand times."

Meanwhile, Edelmann enters another horrible spell of madness. He sneaks out into the night and leaps upon the coach of his servant Ziegfried, who orders his horses to race faster and faster. Edelmann's face leers at him in the darkness.

"Your hands are trembling Ziegfried...You're afraid of me . . . you're afraid I'm going to kill you."

Seconds later, Edelmann pounces on Ziegfried and rips out his throat.

The runaway coach careens into the village, dumping Edelmann into the street. The villagers pour from their homes, and the mob chases the murderer through the town and up the hills and through the cemetery before the madman escapes over the walls of Edelmann's castle. As the scientist tumbles to the ground, Larry Talbot is watching from his window.

Minutes later, Inspector Holtz arrives and demands to see Talbot. Edelmann, having returned to normal, escorts the inspector to Talbot's room but insists that Talbot is guiltless, claiming his recent medical care makes any physical exertion out of the question.

Later that night, Talbot comes to Edelmann's room, tells him that he is aware he murdered Ziegfried and that he wants to help the doctor if he possibly can. Edelmann confides to Talbot the horror of what has befallen him since he feels that the former lycanthrope will understand as others would not. He begs Talbot "Say nothing to Holtz at this time in order to give me time to do for Nina what I've done your you. After that, this evil thing must be destroyed. You have my word that it will be, my boy. But if I'm unable, you must do it for me."

The next night the full moon is about to rise. Edelmann, Miliza and Nina all encourage Talbot who walks alone on the estate ground to confront the rising of the moon. Soon the moon looms over the horizon, and Talbot impulsively raises his hand against his face to block its light. However, he soon realizes that there will be no change, that his curse of lycanthropy is gone and he stands tall, staring at the moon which so terrified him for so many years.

"Doctor, it's wonderful!" rejoices Nina, who turns to find Edelmann has gone. From the laboratory comes the terrible sound of humming electricity. Nina enters the laboratory and sees Edelmann, madly controlling the machinery, rasping at the revived Monster, "I will make you strong. . . stronger than you've ever been. . .the strength of a hundred men . . . !"

"No, Dr. Edelmann," wails Nina. "No! You promised!"

Edelmann spins around and leers at the little hunchback. "You're spying on me . . . you shouldn't have come here . . . I don't like people who see what they're not supposed to see . . ."Grabbing Nina by the throat, he wrenches the life out of the girl and hurls her crooked body into the cave laboratory below.

Down in the village, Steinmuhl has learned that a medical emblem of Edelmann's was found in the hand of his dead brother Ziegfried. He leads a mob of townspeople to the estate, while Holtz alerted of this discovery, marches

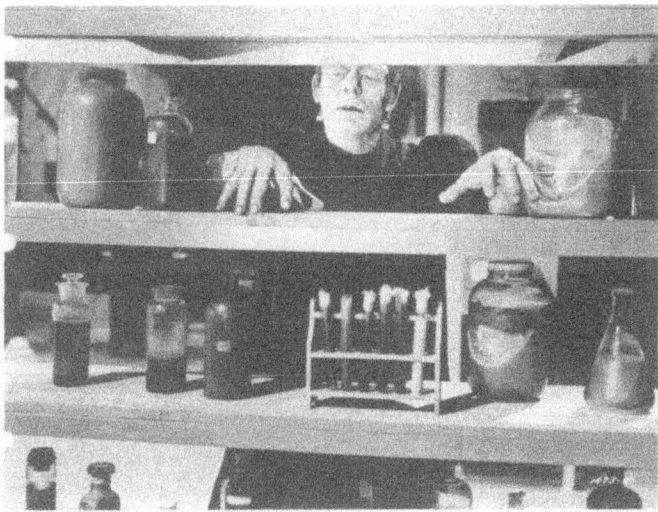

to the castle with two gendarmes. When Nina's scream is heard, Talbot, Miliza and the police run into the laboratory and see the crazed Edelmann and the risen Monster.

The police attack and the Monster pummels them as Edelmann throws Holtz into an electrical dynamo that explodes and roasts the life out of the Inspector.

Reluctantly, Talbot fires two bullets into the man who saved his life and, seconds before death, Edelmann's face shows a sign of peace.

The Monster, outraged that his friend has been slain, goes mad. He lunges for Talbot, who dodges behind a towering shelf of highly combustible chemicals which topples, The castle explodes into flames. "Get out!" shouts Talbot to the villagers who have stormed the castle, "the Frankenstein Monster!" As they run in terror, and Talbot clutches his lovely Miliza, the Monster thrashes about in the flames, finally falling under a massive beam and perishing in the inferno.

THE END

Martha O'Driscoll and Onslow Stevens discuss the final draft of the House of Dracula *script.*

We present, on the following pages, the original final draft
shooting script for House of Dracula

HOUSE OF DRACULA

(DESTINY)

Shooting Script by

Edward T. Lowe

9-20-45.

9-11-45 changes

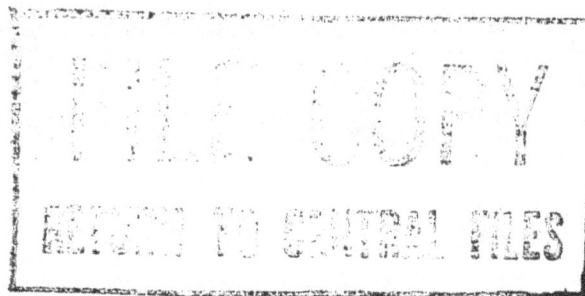

"D E S T I N Y"

FADE IN:

1   INT. MILIZA'S BEDROOM - NIGHT - MED. SHOT

The ANGLE is toward a pair of open French windows through which a giant bat is seen flying across Edelmann's garden toward CAMERA. As it comes into a CLOSE SHOT and hovers toward the window, chittering softly while it looks o.s. with glittering eyes, the CAMERA PANS AWAY to another part of the room where shadows of the creature's wings beat upon the wall beyond the bed in which lies a girl, MILIZA MORELLE. Her face, revealed in the moonlight streaming in through the window, is beautiful. Reacting subconsciously to the o.s. SOUNDS of the bat's chittering, Miliza stirs restively.

2   MED. SHOT - AT WINDOW

The bat's wings beat the air silently for a few seconds longer, while in a DISSOLVE its form melts away into a rapidly attenuating fog which transmutes itself into a man, who, by virtue of his traditional attire, is recognizable as DRACULA. He admires Miliza a moment, then moves away.

3   EXT. EDELMANN'S GARDEN - FULL SHOT

Dracula walks down steps and across the garden toward the French windows of a room on the lower floor.

4   INT. EDELMANN'S STUDY - MED. SHOT

ANGLING into the garden through a French window (closed). Dracula enters, peers through window as CAMERA ANGLES to DOCTOR FRANZ EDELMANN, a man whose face reflects the gentle compassion of one who has devoted his life to helping suffering humanity, is seated in a chair beside his desk, dozing. There is an open book upon the arm of the chair. A large cat, BARTHOLOMEW, is curled upon his lap, asleep.

5   CLOSE SHOT - DRACULA

at the window, his eyes fixed upon Edelmann, o.s. He glances toward book Edelmann has been reading.

5-A   INSERT - BOOK

Its title reads:

        "ADVENTURES IN THE SUPERNATURAL"

6   CLOSEUP - DRACULA

The CAMERA ANGLES with him as he comes through the doorway into --

7   INT. EDELMANN'S STUDY - MED. FULL SHOT

        This WIDER ANGLE reveals that the room is furnished com-
        fortably in the manner of a doctor's office. Dracula,
        entering from the garden terrace, comes down-scene and
        pauses when a little distance from the desk. As he con-
        templates the sleeping man, the cat awakens suddenly...

8   CLOSE SHOT - BARTHOLOMEW

        As the animal looks o.s., its hair bristles. Spitting fear,
        he arches his back, then jumps off Edelmann's lap and runs
        out into the garden...

9   MED. CLOSE SHOT - EDELMANN AND DRACULA

        The sudden movement of the cat jumping from his lap causes
        Edelmann to stir. Edelmann opens his eyes -- staring at
        the intruder.

                         EDELMANN
                What are you doing here! Who are you!?

                         DRACULA
                I am Baron Latos -- I have come to
                you for help ---

                         EDELMANN
                      (he glancess off-
                       stage at clock)
                -- But -- it's five o'clock in the
                morning!

                         DRACULA
                I must apologize for the intrusion.
                But travel for me is extremely difficult
                and I have come a long way.

                         EDELMANN
                I do not understand!

                         DRACULA
                Perhaps you will after you have lead me
                to the basement room of this castle!

                         EDELMANN
                What do you mean?

                         DRACULA
                Have no fear,   octor. Had conditions
                permitted, I would have presented myself
                in the usual manner.

                         EDELMANN
                It is most unusual!

                                        CONTINUED

9   CONTINUED

                              DRACULA
              I will explain everything to you
              before sunrise.

         Edelmann, obviously mystified, follows Dracula toward the
         door --

10   THE GREAT HALL - MED. MOVING SHOT

         Dr. Edelmann lights the candles in a candelabrum and
         proceeds across the hall toward door followed by Dracula.

                              DRACULA
              Dr. Edelmann, do you believe in the
              immortality of the soul?

                              EDELMANN
              I'm a religious man.

                              DRACULA
              Of the body...?

                              EDELMANN
                   (a slight shrug)
              Medical science refutes such a thing.

                              DRACULA
              Just as it denies the existence of
              vampirism?

                              EDELMANN
              It doesn't deny certain physical aspects
              of it. Cases have been recorded in which
              the victims -- driven by some abnormal
              urge, actually believed that blood was
              necessary to keep them alive and became
              psychopathic killers to get it.
                   (professionally)
              These beliefs probably upset their
              metabolism -- brought about chemical
              changes which induced false beliefs and
              lustful appetites.
                   (with a gesture)
              The whole thing is of a highly speculative
              nature -- particularly the supernatural
              aspects.

                              DRACULA
              You doubt the supernatural...?

                              EDELMANN
              -- I find it difficult to believe that
              a human being can change himself into a
              bat, or that by feeding on the blood of
              the living he can attain eternal life.

                                        CONTINUED

10   CONTINUED

They have stopped at the door to the basement stairway which Dr. Edelmann is unlocking. Suddenly he turns to Dracula suspiciously.

> DR. EDELMANN
> But what has this discussion to do
> with us, Baron Latos - ?

> DRACULA
> (cryptically)
> A great deal, perhaps. Shall we proceed,
> Doctor?

Somewhat reluctantly, Edelmann opens the door and they EXIT.

11   INT. BASEMENT ROOM - NIGHT - FULL SHOT

Dr. Edelmann enters carrying a candelabrum. As Dracula and Edelmann descend the stairs, into the room, the CAMERA TRUCKS IN, stopping in a MED. CLOSE SHOT when Edelmann and Dracula reach a point where a coffin of ancient pattern rests upon a couple of broken blocks of masonry. Edelmann reacts.

12   CLOSE SHOT - EDELMANN AND DRACULA

Edelmann, startled, is staring at the coffin.

> EDELMANN
> The Dracula Crest !

Dracula , smiling slightly, extends his right hand and points to the ring he wears.

13   CLOSE SHOT - DRACULA'S HANDS

The large ring on his second finger carries a crested Coat of Arms, that of the House of Dracula.

14   CLOSEUP - DRACULA

> DRACULA
> (quietly)
> Yes, Doctor... you see before you a man
> who has lived for centuries -- kept alive
> by the blood of innocent people.

15   MED. CLOSE TWO SHOT

> EDELMANN
> (with a skeptical smile)
> You ask me to believe that?

> DRACULA
> (pleadingly)
> That is why I've come here -- to seek
> release from a curse of misery and horror
> against which I am powerless to fight alone.

16   CLOSE SHOT - EDELMANN

Intrigued, Edelmann takes a few steps toward the coffin.

                    EDELMANN
          According to legend, a vampire must
          return to his grave before sun up. If
          you were to remain here, how would that
          be possible?

16-A   TWO SHOT - EDELMANN AND DRACULA

                    DRACULA
          Within this coffin is a layer of soil
          taken from my birthplace... That earth
          makes this my grave -- in which I must
          lie helpless during the daylight hours.

                    EDELMANN
                  (tolerantly)
          Because one ray of sunlight falling
          upon a vampire would destroy him --?

                    DRACULA
          Yes, Doctor...

Edelmann looks toward the direction of their entrance, and
then at Dracula with a return of his annoyance and
resentment.

                    EDELMANN
          The door of this room was locked...
                  (indicating coffin)
          How did you get this in here?

                    DRACULA
                  (smiling slightly)
          Since you do not believe in the super-
          natural, let us say that you were
          mistaken, that the outer door was not
          locked.

                    EDELMANN
          You've taken a great deal for granted,
          Baron... Proceeding on the assumption
          that I would take your case.

                    DRACULA
          Your reputation for helping others
          made me certain that you would...

A glint of shrewd calculation comes into Dracula's eyes
as he draws closer to Edelmann.

17   CLOSER SHOT - THE TWO

                          DRACULA
              Whatever the cause of my
              condition, could you effect
              a cure?

                          EDELMANN
              There might be a way -- despite
              the dangers involved --- It
              would be a challenge to medical
              science -

                          DRACULA
              Accept the challenge, Doctor!
              Release me from this curse of
              misery and horror -- against
              which I am powerless to fight
              alone!

        Edelmann stands pondering the subject without answering
        as Dracula glances toward the casement window. Half
        turning, he gestures toward it.

                          DRACULA
              You must decide quickly,
              Doctor -- before the dawn.

        While Edelmann is still debating the subject, the CAMERA
        LEAVES them, PANNING UP to the casement window showing a
        shaft of light which foretells the approach of dawn as
        we DISSOLVE OUT.

18   INT. EDELMANN'S RECEPTION HALL - DAY - FULL SHOT

        As Edelmann enters through the doorway upscene from the
        stairs, the CAMERA IS TRUCKING FORWARD so that he and
        the three people who are entering from the main part of
        the room are in a MED. GROUP SHOT when the MOVEMENT
        STOPS. Two of the group are a peasant-type woman and
        her son, JOHANNES, a lad of seven. The third person
        whose face is not seen immediately, is Miliza. She
        wears nurse's attire.

                          MILIZA
              Good morning, Doctor...

                                              CONTINUED

18   CONTINUED

>   EDELMANN
>   Good morning, Miliza... Well,
>   Johannes! How's that leg?

He stoops in front of the lad as the CAMERA MOVES UP.

>   JOHANNES
>   It's fine since you made it long
>   like my other one! I can learn
>   to ski now, can't I?

Edelmann bends the lad's knee a couple of times.

>   EDELMANN
>   Does that hurt?

>   JOHANNES
>   Not as much as it did...

>   EDELMANN
>   Then maybe we'll go skiing
>   together --
>   (winking assuringly)
>   -- this winter...

>   JOHANNES
>   Did you hear what he said, Mommie!?
>   I can go skiing!

He dances around his mother, who is dabbing her eyes.

>   MOTHER
>   Doctor -- I can't tell you --
>   (choking up)
>   -- how much it means --

>   EDELMANN
>   Now, now ... Goodbye, Johannes...
>   (he hands the lad
>   a coin)
>   To buy candy with...

>   JOHANNES
>   Come on, Mommie! Come on!

His mother, too full of gratitude for words, permits
the lad to pull her toward the door...

19   CLOSE SHOT - EDELMANN

He looks after the boy, smiling, then moves toward
another part of the reception hall in a PAN SHOT which
brings Miliza into view, revealing for the first time
that she is girl upon whom Dracula (as the bat) gazed
the night before.

CONTINUED

19   CONTINUED

                              MILIZA
                    She asked about your fee...

                              EDELMANN
                    Let's forget it a while... She'll
                    pay something now and then --
                    whenever she can...

As Edelmann exits toward his study, Miliza looks after
him for a moment with a smile which indicates that his
answer is what she guessed it might be, then moves to
where one of the castle's tables has been impressed
into service as a receiving desk. On it are a couple
of small index boxes. Nearby is a four-drawer letter
file and a typewriter -- modern articles (for the
period) in contrast to the rest of the castle's
medieval atmosphere. As she sits at her desk to
take up the routine of the morning's work, CUT TO -

20   THE LABORATORY AND SURGERY

          -- a large room, which for the period is furnished
          with the finest equipment available. There are two
          operating tables, together with the usual instrument
          cases and stands. The far end of the room exhibits an
          elaborate array of high-frequency apparatus: a large
          Oudin coil, a portable switchboard, a motor-generator,
          a rotating spark-gap, etc. There are French windows
          which open into the garden terrace. Opposite these a
          part of the wall has been altered to accommodate a large
          refrigeration unit which has been converted into a
          temperature and humidity controlled incubator, for
          scientific purposes. The steam unit for this is an auto-
          clave, from which pipes pass through the woodwork into
          the interior of the chamber. In this are growing some
          strangely formed plants, which will be described later.

          Seated at a laboratory table in f.g., is a girl engaged
          in gathering some mold from a "slant" culture tube by
          means of a platinum loop. On this same table is a
          brass-finished microscope. (Period of about 1880).

          The girl, NINA, wears a technician's white smock. She
          is slight of build and undeniably lovely, but one whose
          expression reflects a certain tragic quality. She is
          concentrating on maneuvering the loop through the neck
          of the culture tube as Edelmann reaches her.

                              EDELMANN
                    What progress, Nina?

                              NINA
                    Splendid, Doctor!

                                                    CONTINUED

20   CONTINUED

She touches the mold on the loop to the surface of
the jellied agar-agar in a Petri dish and, after
covering it, springs to her feet. As she does
so, it is seen that she is deformed, a hunchback.

                    NINA
                (continuing)
          I increased the humidity in
          the incubator as you suggested,
          and the spores are multiplying
          faster than ever...

                    EDELMANN
          Good!

From his pocket he takes a four-ounce vial
containing a dark-colored liquid and hands it
to her.

                    EDELMANN
                (continuing)
          Blood smear.

He picks up the culture tube and inspects the mold.

                    EDELMANN
                (continuing)
          We're making progress...

                    NINA
          The operation on Johannes' leg
          proves that...

During this, she has opened the bottle...

21   CLOSEUP - NINA'S HAND

The label on the bottle carries the following legend
in hand-printed letters:

               BLOOD SPECIMEN
                 -- Baron Latos

Nina's right hand comes into the picture and by
means of the glass rod she holds, extracts a drop
of blood from the bottle. Over this:

                    NINA'S VOICE
                (continued)
          If we succeed in producing the
          mold in quantity --

22   MED. CLOSE SHOT - EDELMANN AND NINA

Nina puts the bottle down and transfers the drop of blood
to the center of a glass "slip" as she continues:

                    NINA
          -- think what it will mean to
          thousands of people throughout
          the world...

                    EDELMANN
          And to you. We'll succeed, Nina
          -- and when we do, I'll make you
          stand erect -- with a back that
          is straight -- and strong...

Made silent by her emotions, Nina picks up a "cover
glass" and dexterously draws one of its edges along the
slip, thus spreading the blood into a "smear." During
this, Edelmann sits at the table and places the microscope
in front of the light, his business of adjusting the
mirror being completed by the time Nina finishes the
slide by using a small pipette to place a few drops of a
staining solution upon it from a small bottle. Dipping
the slide into a beaker of water to rinse off the super-
fluous color, she drops a clean "cover glass" into position in its center and hands it to Edelmann.

23   CLOSE SHOT - EDELMANN

Placing the slide under the fingers of the microscope
stage, Edelmann touches the "cover glass" with a drop of
cedar oil from a small bottle and focuses the "oil immer-
sion" lens slowly into position while looking through the
eyepiece.

24   CLOSE SHOT - BLOOD SLIDE

Revealed by high magnification, the red and white corpuscles are clearly seen. Among them are peculiarly
shaped parasitic microbes -- perhaps in the form of Try-
panosoma, whose pseudopods appear to envelop the red
corpuscles.

25   CLOSE SHOT - EDELMANN AND NINA

Edelmann, made thoughtful by what he sees, looks up at
Nina and indicates the bottle.

                    EDELMANN
          Make a culture from this and
          prepare an anti-toxin as soon
          as possible.

Deeply puzzled, he is peering into the microscope again
as the scene -
                                        FADES OUT

FADE IN:

26   INT. BASEMENT ROOM - DAY - CLOSE SHOT - WINDOW

The CAMERA PANS ALONG a slanting beam of sunlight until it stops in a MED. SHOT of Dracula's coffin. The gradually dying light stretches out longer and longer until, as the sun sets, it disappears entirely. The lid of the coffin begins to rise slowly. As Dracula's groping fingers appear, clutching the edge of the box,

DISSOLVE INTO

27   THE GREAT HALL - NIGHT - MED. SHOT - DOORS

The jangling of an o.s. bell is HEARD. Nina, just reaching the foot of the stairs, turns into the reception hall and opens the door. Dracula is standing there.

>   DRACULA
>   Good evening...I am Baron Latos--

28   ANOTHER PART OF THE ROOM - MED. SHOT - TOWARD ENTRANCE HALL

Miliza, attired in an informal dinner dress, is seated on the sofa reading, picked up in a surprised and pleased reaction as she hears:
>   DRACULA'S VOICE
>   (continuing)
>   -- Doctor Edelmann is expecting me...

>   NINA'S VOICE
>   Oh yes, Baron... Come in, please...

Smiling, Miliza hurries toward the hallway, where Nina is ushering Dracula into the main part of the room.

29   CLOSE SHOT - ANGLING INTO RECEPTION HALL

Dracula, seeing Miliza, stops short with a manner of surprise and pleasure which equals her.

>   DRACULA
>   Morelle!

Nina, seeing that the new patient and Miliza know each other, reacts with mild surprise and exits through the upscene doors.

>   DRACULA
>   (continues)
>   A most pleasant surprise...

CONTINUED

bv

29   CONTINUED

                        MILIZA
            It's good to see you again...

Dracula bends over her hand for an instant during which
it is evident that she is pleased.

                        DRACULA
            You left Bistritz just as we
            were becoming acquainted.

                        MILIZA
            When the opportunity arose for
            me to become Doctor Edelmann's
            assistant, I couldn't refuse...

                        DRACULA
                    (warmly)
            Now that chance has brought us
            together again, I hope to see
            you quite often...

                        MILIZA
            You're not here as a patient...?

                        DRACULA
            Unfortunately...

Edelmann is appearing down the stairway as:

                        DRACULA
                    (continues)
            The doctor thought it advisable
            that I come here for treatment...

                        EDELMANN
            Ah -- Baron... I've been expecting
            you...
                    (to Miliza)
            It will be necessary that Baron
            Latos have his appointments during
            the evenings...
                    (to Dracula)
            We'll go to my study...

Dracula bows to Miliza and exits with Edelmann.

30   CLOSE SHOT - MILIZA

As she looks after them, it is apparent that she is
pleased by Dracula's interest.

31   EDELMANN'S STUDY -- MED. SHOT

Edelmann and Dracula enter from the Great Hall, Edelmann
indicates a chair near his desk.

> EDELMANN
>
> Sit down...

> DRACULA
>
> Thank you.

The CAMERA MOVES UP. Dracula, in the sincere, intent
manner of a patient, waits for Edelmann to speak. Edelmann
frowns thoughtfully.

> EDELMANN
>
> It appears that I may have to
> alter my theories... An examina-
> tion of your blood reveals the
> presence of a peculiar parasite
> -- a form with which I am com-
> pletely unfamiliar. It's possible
> that they have something to do
> with your problem, and proceeding
> on the assumption that they have --

He walks thoughtfully to and fro near the table

> EDELMANN
> (continuing)
> -- I am having an anti-toxin
> prepared, so that we can see...

> DRACULA
>
> Your new theory being...?

> EDELMANN
>
> Basically, Louis Pasteur's --
> that a pure culture of a parasite,
> introduced into the parent blood-
> stream, will set upon and destroy
> not only its own kind, but them-
> selves as well...

> DRACULA
> (impressed)
> It sounds rather promising...

> EDELMANN
>
> Perhaps... But we must proceed
> slowly --

> DRACULA
>
> The treatments will take some time?

CONTINUED

31   CONTINUED

> EDELMANN
> Without doubt...
> (his manner conveys
> a veiled warning)
> Meanwhile, your visits here are
> to be made only at intervals --
> on the nights and at the hours I
> shall designate. Is that under-
> stood?

> DRACULA
> Quite clearly.

> EDELMANN
> Then the treatments will begin
> tonight -- with a transfusion.

> DRACULA
> A transfusion?

> EDELMANN
> It will help you temporarily --
> while the anti-toxin is being
> prepared...

As he says this, the scene is -

DISSOLVING INTO

32   EXT. ENTRANCE OF EDELMANN'S HOME - <u>NIGHT</u> - MED. CLOSE
SHOT - DOORS

LAWRENCE TALBOT, a well set up fellow in his thirties, is
banging the knocker vigorously. His face reflects tragedy.
He is obviously in the grip of emotions which he controls
only by the greatest effort...

33   INT. EDELMANN'S RECEPTION HALL - MED. SHOT

Miliza appears from the Great Hall simultaneously with
Seigfried's entrance from another direction. Reacting
to the continued and more insistent sounds of the knocker,
Miliza pauses near the entrance while Seigfried opens the
door. Talbot almost bursts into the room. Seeing Miliza,
he addresses her.

> TALBOT
> I must see Doctor Edelmann, at once!

As Miliza steps forward, Seigfried exists and the CAMERA
MOVES UP CLOSER.

CONTINUED

33   CONTINUED

                         MILIZA
                    (apologetically)
               He's engaged just now.

                         TALBOT
               For how long!?

Miliza, reacting to his tense manner and the deep strain
in his voice, is gently sympathetic.

                         MILIZA
               Some little time, I'm afraid...

                         TALBOT
                    (taking a step
                     forward)
               Can't you interrupt him? I've
               come a long way--
                    (almost pleadingly)
               Tell him my name - Talbot! Lawrence
               Talbot! Maybe he'll understand!

                         MILIZA
               I'm sorry, but that's impossible.
               He giving a transfusion...

Talbot's fingers dig deeply into the palms of his hands.

                         TALBOT
               How long will that take--an hour?

                         MILIZA
               At least that,...
                    (indicating the
                     Great Hall)
               If you'd care to wait...

Talbot's emotions break leash.

                         TALBOT
               I can't wait! There isn't time!
                    (turning precipi-
                     tately toward the
                     door)
               There isn't time!

He flings himself out into the night. Miliza, puzzled,
but with sympathy evident in her manner, steps to the
open door. The CAMERA MOVES UP CLOSER as she stands there
looking after Talbot's exit while the scene -

                                        DISSOLVES INTO

34   INT. SURGERY, LABORATORY - NIGHT - MED. CLOSE

Dracula, wearing one of Edelmann's surgical coats, is
standing beside an operating table. One of his sleeves
is rolled up and Nina is swabbing the crook of his arm
with a cotton pat.

                         NINA
                    (finishing the
                    business)
          There...

                         DRACULA
          Thank you.

Nina steps away in a PAN SHOT which brings Edelmann into
view, lying upon a second operating table. His eyes are
closed and he is holding a cotton pat on the crook of his
exposed arm. Nina, with a little frown, pours a stimulant into a glass and steps closer to the table.

                         NINA
          Drink this, Doctor -- it'll make
          you feel better...

As Edelmann sits up with a nod and a smile and drinks the
stimulant, the CAMERA PULLS BACK INTO A LARGER SHOT.
During the interval, Dracula has removed the surgeon's
coat and donned his own.

                         EDELMANN
          Your next appointment is for
          Thursday evening, Baron...

                         DRACULA
          At about the same time...
                    (to Nina)
          Good night... Good night, Doctor...

He starts toward the door of Edelmann's study, through
which Miliza is entering. As they pass, Dracula bows
and continues his exit, while Miliza comes down to where
Nina is now assisting Edelmann out of his surgeon's coat.

                         MILIZA
          A Mr. Talbot was here to
          see you, Doctor, He seemed
          very upset.

                         EDELMANN
          Talbot?

CONTINUED

34   CONTINUED

                    MILIZA
          Lawrence Talbot. He thought you'd
          recognize the name.
                    (compassionately)
          There was something tragic in his
          face, Doctor -- the look of a man
          tormented by fear. When I told him
          you were busy, he rushed out of the
          house saying that he couldn't wait,
          that there wouldn't be time...

                    EDELMANN
                    (reflectively)
          Talbot? Perhaps he'll come back..

The telephone rings. Nina answers.

                    NINA
          Hello...
                    (pause)
          Just a moment, please...
                    (to Edelmann)
          It's Inspector Holtz...

                    EDELMANN
                    (taking phone)
          Yes, Inspector...?
                    (after pause, dur-
                    ing which he frowns)
          Very well, I'll come down...

                    EDELMANN
                    (indicating his
                    satchel)
          You'd better come along, Miliza

                    NINA
                    (concerned)
          You should rest, after giving a
          transfusion.

                    EDELMANN
          Holtz says it's urgent!

Miliza is following Edelmann toward the door as the
scene -

                                        DISSOLVES INTO

ae

35   EXT. VISARIA SIDE STREET - NIGHT - FULL SHOT

A buggy is being driven rapidly down a side street toward
the corner. As the vehicle reaches f.g., the CAMERA
ANGLES with it so that the street lamp reveals Edelmann,
driving, and Miliza seated beside him. The CHANGING ANGLE
now discloses Visaria's main avenue, at the far end of
which a group of people are gathered in front of --

36   POLICE HEADQUARTERS

--before which Edelmann reins his horse to a stop. As he
and Meliza alight in med. f.g., the excited villagers are
arguing with HOFFMAN, a policeman whose uniformed bulk
bars their entrance into the building. Among the group,
one named STEINMUHL is the most insistent.

                    AD LIBS
          Steinmuhl: Why can't we go in?
          Hoffman: Inspector Holtz says you can't!
          Steinmuhl: We've as much right as anyone else!
          Hoffman: Stand back now! Stand back!
          Villager: Here's Doctor Edelmann!
          Steinmuhl: Can we go in with you, Doctor?
          Second
          Villager: I want to see what he looks like...
          Third
          Villager: So do I!
          Steinmuhl: We've got our wives and children
                      to think of...

Edelmann and Miliza are now close to the entrance. As
they pass through the doorway, the villagers surge forward
but are stopped again by Hoffman.

37   INT. POLICE HEADQUARTERS - MED. CLOSE SHOT - ENTRANCE

INSPECTOR HOLTZ, a rather pompous man in his middle forties,
is reaching the doorway.

                    HOLTZ
          Good evening, Doctor -- Miss
          Morello...
                    (calling through
                    the doorway)
          You people go home!
                    (to Edelmann)
          If I find the one who told that
          we had a crazy man here, I'll lock
          him up!

The CAMERA PRECEDES the trio into the room, at the far
end of which is a desk behind which sits a sergeant.

                                        CONTINUED

                    HOLTZ
                 (continues)
        He came in a little while ago and
        demanded that I put him in a cell
        -- to keep him from committing
        murder, he said. I did it -- to
        humor him -- but when he started
        raving, I knew we had something
        serious on our hands and sent for
        you... Appears to be a --

The MOVEMENT has brought them to a door on the right.

                    HOLTZ
                 (continues)
        -- a rather decent sort, other-
        wise... Name of Talbot...

                    EDELMANN
        Talbot... Talbot...

                    MILIZA
        You remember, Doctor... the young
        man I told you about ...

                    HOLTZ
                 (opening the door)
        He's in here...

38   INT. CELL CORRIDOR - MED. CLOSE SHOT - DOOR

As Holtz, Edelmann and Miliza enter, the CAMERA SWINGS
AWAY to show a cell, barred across its entire front.
Talbot, within the cell, is standing at the door. There
is fury in his voice as he looks off toward those who are
entering.
                    TALBOT
        I didn't come here to be exhibited --

The CAMERA IS PULLING BACK into a GROUP SHOT as -

                    TALBOT
                 (continues)
        -- like a monkey on a stick! Get
        those people out of here!

                    HOLTZ
        Take it easy, now... This is Doctor
        Edelmann... You wanted to see him,
        didn't you!?
                    TALBOT
                 (to Edelmann)
        That's why I came to Visaria -- in
        the hope that you might help me.
        But you're too late! No one can
        help me now... There isn't time...

CONTINUED

38   CONTINUED

                              EDELMANN
                            (quietly)
                Tell me   what troubles you...

                              TALBOT
                Do you believe a human being can
                turn into a beast?

Miliza is shocked. Edelmann studies Talbot's eyes.

                              EDELMANN
                Anything can happen -- in a
                person's mind...

                              TALBOT
                This isn't in my mind!

He thrusts his arm through the bars as he continues:

                              TALBOT
                Look at that! Do you know what
                it is!?

39   CLOSE SHOT - TALBOT'S FOREARM

On the underside is seen a five-pointed star, somewhat in
the nature of a birthmark. Over this is heard:

                            TALBOT'S VOICE
                It's the pentagram --

40   INSIDE CELL - MED. CLOSE SHOT - ANGLING INTO CORRIDOR

                              TALBOT
                  (continues)
                -- the mark of the beast! When
                the full moon rises, I become a
                 werewolf -- with only one desire
                in my mind -- to kill!

41   CORRIDOR - GROUP SHOT - ANGLING INTO CELL

Miliza stares incredulously toward Talbot, who is moving
toward the window.

                              EDELMANN
                Talbot! The pentagram means
                nothing...!

42   CELL - CLOSE SHOT - SIDE ANGLE ON TALBOT - AT WINDOW

He is looking out into the night as:

                            EDELMANN'S VOICE
                  (continues)
                It's only a stigmatic mark, induced
                hypnotically by what you believe...!

43   EXT. LONG SHOT - OVER HOUSE TOPS - (SPECIAL EFFECT)

       The rim of the moon appears above the gaunt silhouettes
       of the buildings, softening them in its bathing light.

44   INT. CELL - ANGLING FROM EXTERIOR THROUGH WINDOW

       Talbot, moving as though drawn by some irresistible
       force, steps full into the moonlight. As he does so, the
       transmuting change begins, bringing an expression over
       his face which is half-human, half-bestial.

                         EDELMANN'S VOICE
                          (commandingly)
                  Listen to me, Talbot! There's no
                  such thing as a werewolf!

45   MED. SHOT - ANGLING INTO CELL

       Holtz crosses himself. Miliza watches with fascinated
       horror, hardly able to credit what is taking place.

                           EDELMANN
                          (continues)
                  It's a belief that exists only
                  in your mind!

46   CELL - MED. CLOSE SHOT - TALBOT

       On his hands and face is appearing a hairy growth...

47   CORRIDOR - HOLTZ, EDELMANN AND MELIZA

       Meliza stares, mute with horror. Holtz, moistening his
       dry lips, stands rooted to the spot. Edelmann, shocked
       into silence, watches Talbot with the interest of a
       scientist and the sympathy of a doctor.

48   CELL - CLOSE SHOT - TALBOT

       As the transformation continues, Talbot bares his teeth,
       which have become fang-like. Now, dominated by the
       savage instincts which have possessed him, he moves in
       a PAN SHOT which brings him to the bars. Glaring at
       those in the corridor, he rattles the door...

49   CORRIDOR - GROUP SHOT

       Holtz draws back, paralyzed by fear. Miliza, with deep
       sympathy, closes her eyes to shut out the horror...

50   CELL - CLOSE SHOT - TALBOT

       Enraged into animal savagery, he flings himself away in
       a PAN SHOT, becoming now something that is human in form
       but inhuman in appearance, a pitiful thing which hurls
       itself violently upon the floor and lies there, snarling.

51   CORRIDOR - CLOSE SHOT - EDELMANN AND MILIZA

       Miliza's eyes glisten as she turns to Edelmann.

                           MILIZA
             Isn't there something you can do...?

                           EDELMANN
                         (quietly)
             Not until morning -- when this has
             passed.
                         (to Holtz)
             Bring him to me then... Put him in
             my care and I'll do all that I can...

       Miliza, not daring to look again upon Talbot's suffering,
       buries her face against Edelmann's shoulder. Edelmann,
       exhibiting sympathy, looks through the bars into the --

52   CELL - MED. CLOSE SHOT

       Talbot, groveling upon the floor, lies there panting,
       consumed by the violence of his bestial seizure...

                                          DISSOLVE TO

53   OMITTED
thru
60

61   EXT. EDELMANN'S GARDEN - MED. SHOT - DAY

       Long shadows stretch out over the grass-grown flagstones,
       cast there by the rays of the late afternoon sun shining
       through the lacework of the blossom-laden apple trees.
       On the right is an open iron stairway which leads upward
       to Miliza's bedroom.

       Talbot is seated upon a bench some distance upscene, his
       head resting dejectedly upon his upturned hands.

62   MED. CLOSE SHOT - TERRACE

       Miliza, attired in nurse's white, but without cap, enters
       to Great Hall. She looks off toward Talbot with compas-
       sionate understanding before she moves into the garden
       in a PAN SHOT which brings him into view.

63   MED. CLOSE SHOT - BENCH

Miliza, entering quietly, regards Talbot with a sympathetic smile before she speaks:

                    MILIZA
          Mr. Talbot...

Talbot springs to his feet, startled. The tragic lines which etch his face soften into a strained smile.

                    TALBOT
          I didn't hear you...

Miliza adopts a cheery manner, to convey encouragement.

                    MILIZA
          That's all right...

Talbot's next words are almost a prayer.

                    TALBOT
          Do you think -- that Doctor Edel-
          mann can help me?

                    MILIZA
          He's done some wonderful things...

                    TALBOT
          Then why has he kept me waiting
          all day!? Doesn't he know that
          tonight --
                    (controlling
                    himself)
          I'm sorry... I know he'll do
          whatever he can...

                    MILIZA
                  (assuringly)
          He wants to see you now...

Talbot, tensely hopeful, joins Miliza in a PAN SHOT which takes them toward the terrace as the scene -

                                        DISSOLVES INTO

64   INT. LABORATORY HUMIDITY ROOM - DAY - FULL SHOT

This is from within the converted refrigeration unit, ANGLING into the laboratory. On several small tables there are numerous shallow boxes -- hot-house "flats" in which are growing a number of plants, hybrid forms of Clavaria Formosa, a spore producing growth whose "tree coral" characteristics remind one somewhat of desert Joshuas.

                                        CONTINUED

64   CONTINUED

Above each of the tables is a cone-shaped reflector,
casting light and warmth downward. Edelmann, in close
f.g., is inspecting the thermometer and humidity indi-
cator, turning from them to open the steam control valve
a bit more just as Miliza and Talbot come into view, in
the laboratory. They join Nina, who is seated at her
table engaged in transfering mold from a culture flask
to the agar-agar into a Petri dish. Edelmann, seeing
Talbot, breaks a stem from one of the plants and exits
into --

65   LABORATORY - MAIN ROOM

-- where Talbot and Miliza are waiting as Edelmann comes
from the humidity room and joins them.

                    EDELMANN
          Ah, Mr. Talbot...

Talbot is taut and tense.

                    TALBOT
          You've something to tell me?

                    EDELMANN
          Well, yes -- I have...
                    (professionally)
          The examination we made this morn-
          ing discloses a most unusual condi-
          tion -- an over-all pressure upon
          the brain, due to the fact that its
          cavity hasn't enlarged proportionately
          to its growth...
                    (brief pause)
          This condition, coupled with your
          belief that the moon can bring about
          a change, accomplishes exactly
          that... During the period in which
           your reasoning processes give way
          to self-hypnosis, the glands which
          govern your metabolism --

66   CLOSE SHOT - TALBOT AND MILIZA

Talbot tenses forward. Miliza rests her hand upon his
arm in an impulsive, restraining gesture.

                    EDELMANN'S VOICE
                    (continued)
          -- got out of control, like a
          steam engine without a balance wheel.
          When this happens, the glands generate
          an abnormal supply of certain hormones--

67   GROUP SHOT

                              EDELMANN
                           (continued)
                    -- in your case, those which bring
                    about the physical transformation
                    you experience.

                              TALBOT
                           (challengingly)
                    Explaining it doesn't help! What
                    can you do about it!? Operate?

                              EDELMANN
                    An operation to enlarge the cranial
                    cavity is too dangerous to attempt...

                              TALBOT
                    Then there's nothing you can do!?

                              EDELMANN
                    I didn't say that... Under certain
                    conditions -- which we've tried to
                    duplicate in there --

He indicates the humidity room, then exhibits the stem he
holds in his hand:

                              EDELMANN
                           (continued)
                    -- this plant produces a mold from
                    which we've been able to distill --
                    well, a substance which possesses
                    the property of softening any hard
                    structure composed of calcium salts
                    ... bone, for instance.

68   CLOSE SHOT - EDELMANN AND NINA

Nina's eyes begin to light up as:

                              EDELMANN
                           (continues)
                    With this medium, many things are
                    possible...
                              (a gentle smile
                              toward Nina)
                    Help for Nina...

69   GROUP SHOT
                              EDELMANN
                           (to Talbot)
                    -- and for you also -- by the same
                    process which will permit your
                    brain -- without an operation --
                    to reshape the cranial cavity and
                    thus overcome the pressure...

                                        CONTINUED

69   CONTINUED

TALBOT
You can do this now!?

Miliza and Nina glance at each other. They know of the
difficulties which lie ahead. Talbot reacts to
Edelmann's momentary silence.

TALBOT
Can you!?

EDELMANN
(frowning)
These plants are difficult to
grow... It will take time to produce the mold in sufficient quantity...

Talbot grasps Edelmann's arm.

TALBOT
The full moon will rise in an hour!
Isn't there something you can do now!?

EDELMANN
(gently)
Only what you did for yourself last
night -- confine you...

TALBOT
I can't go through it again!

He flings himself away and runs toward the garden exit.
Miliza, recovering from the shock of Talbot's reaction,
unconsciously uses his first name as she runs after him.

MILIZA
Larry! Come back!

Edelmann follows her.

70   EXT. GARDEN - MED. PAN SHOT

This PICKS TALBOT UP as he enters from the house and runs
across the garden past Seigfried, who is trimming a hedge,
and then on toward the gate...

71   MED. CLOSE SHOT - TERRACE

Miliza and Edelmann appear from the laboratory. Reacting
with hardly a pause, they start out after Talbot.

ae

72   MED. SHOT - GATE

      Talbot is disappearing through the gate into...

73   OUTSIDE EDELMANN'S CASTLE WALL - FULL SHOT (MAT)

      On the left, in f.g., there is an irregularity in the
      cliff's more or less straight contour -- a shallow,
      canyon-like break whose sheer, smooth sides form a well-
      like caldron known as "The Devil's Hole." Talbot is
      running blindly toward its edge.

74   EDELMANN'S GARDEN - MED. SHOT

      Miliza and Edelmann pass Seigfried, who looks curiously
      after them as they exit through the gate...

75   OUTSIDE EDELMANN'S CASTLE WALL - MED. CLOSE - AT GATE

      Miliza and Edelmann appear, pausing as they see --

76   MED. LONG SHOT - OVER DEVIL'S HOLE

      Talbot, running toward f.g., reaches the brink...

77   OUTSIDE CASTLE WALL - CLOSE SHOT - MILIZA AND EDELMANN

      Horror comes into their eyes as they see Talbot.

                              EDELMANN
            (Talbot!
            (
            (MILIZA
            (Larry! Larry!

      They start out in his direction.

78   INT. MED. SHOT - FROM INSIDE DEVIL'S HOLE

      -- ANGLING UPWARD ON Talbot as he looks down into --

79   EXT. DEVIL'S HOLE - FULL DOWNWARD SHOT

      This reveals the well's sheer, smooth sides. The boom-
      ing waves form a whirling maelstrom, whose overflow finds
      an outlet through a low opening in the rock just above
      the water level.

80   CLOSE SHOT - TALBOT - ON BRINK

He is frantic, beseiged by tormenting thoughts of the horror which the fast approaching night will bring.

81   FULL SHOT - ACROSS DEVIL'S HOLE TOWARD CASTLE

Miliza and Edelmann are running toward Talbot...

82   INT. DEVIL'S HOLE - ANGLING UPWARD ON TALBOT

-- as he leaps forward over the Camera into --

83   EXT. THE DEVIL'S HOLE

-- in a DOWNWARD ANGLE which shows Talbot's body plunging into the churning water.

84   -- ANGLING UPWARD on Miliza and Edelmann on the brink. They are horrified, helpless...

85   MAELSTROM IN DEVIL'S HOLE - MED. SHOT

Talbot is being swept into the mouth of the cave.

86   CLOSE SHOT - MILIZA AND EDELMANN - ON BRINK

Miliza chokes a sob and buries her face in her hands. Edelmann calls toward the castle with purpose and decision in his voice:

                    EDELMANN
        Seigfried! Seigfried!
          (turns to Miliza)
        -- The ground below us is honey-
        combed with caves made by the
        ocean tides -- there is still
        hope that Talbot can be saved.

As he talks the scene

                                DISSOLVES INTO

87   EXT. DEVIL'S HOLE - ANGLING TOWARD CASTLE - <u>NIGHT</u>

The moon is about midway between the zenith and the horizon. On the left of the hole, Miliza and Edelmann are standing near its edge while a little distance from them, Seigfried and Steinmuhl are completing an arrangement of ropes which stretch across it.

                                CONTINUED

87   CONTINUED

The largest of these ropes is strung tightly between two
braces, one on either side. The second rope which passes
through the lower wheel of a double pulley, is fastened
to a "Bosun's chair." By means of this rope, the chair
can be raised and lowered... The upper wheel of the pulley
rides along the main rope. Other and smaller ropes are
attached to the shackle of the pulley, so that the chair
may be drawn out and pulled back along the supporting rope,
in traverse fashion...

                                              WIPE TO

88   NEAR DEVIL'S HOLE - CLOSE SHOT - SIEGFRIED AND STEINMUHL

They pull together on the block and tackle which tightens
the main rope, then hang on it for a second to test its
tautness...

89   CLOSE SHOT - EDELMANN AND MILIZA - NEAR BRINK OF HOLE

Edelmann, hauling the Bosun's chair to the brink of the
Hole, straightens out and arranges its various ropes.
Miliza, nearby, unstraps the buckles of a flat-cork life
belt. During this, Steinmuhl enters and goes to Edelmann.

90   CLOSE SHOT - STEINMUHL AND EDELMANN

                         STEINMUHL
                We're ready, Doctor...

Edelmann glances at him...Miliza enters.

91   CLOSE SHOT - EDELMANN

He frowns slightly as he looks off toward --

92   MED. LONG SHOT - TOWARD EDELMANN'S CASTLE

There is still quite some distance between the moon and
the horizon...

93   CLOSE SHOT - EDELMANN, STEINMUHL AND MILIZA - NEAR BRINK

Miliza is watching Edelmann, reacting to his frown as he
turns to Steinmuhl.

                                              CONTINUED

"DESTINY" - Changes 9/20/45

CONTINUED

EDELMANN
Tell Seigfried we'll wait awhile...

Steinmuhl looks at Edelmann a second and then, with a
slight shrug, exits. Edelmann, seeing Miliza's equally
puzzled manner, explains:

EDELMANN
If Talbot's been swept into the
caves down there, he's still the
Wolfman -- and will remain so until
the moon sets ---

MILIZA
And when it does, he'll try to kill
himself again!

EDELMANN
(assuringly)
Unless I find him just as the seizure
passes, and persuade him to live --

Miliza, understanding, bites her lip and looks away...

94   CLOSE SHOT - STEINMUHL AND SEIGFRIED

STEINMUHL
(disgruntled)
We work half the night to get this
thing rigged up, and then he says
we'll wait... What's going on here,
anyway...?

SEIGFRIED
That's Doctor Edelmann's business.

STEINMUHL
Strange business, if you ask me...

He looks off suspiciously toward Edelmann as the scene

DISSOLVES INTO

95   MED. LONG SHOT - TOWARD EDELMANN'S CASTLE - (STOCK)

The moon is only a little distance above the horizon.

96   EXT. BRINK OF DEVIL'S HOLE - CLOSE SHOT - EDELMANN AND
MILIZA

Edelmann, now in the Bosun's seat, is wearing the life
belt and Miliza is handing him a lighted lantern.

EDELMANN
(calling off)
Stand by --

97   MED. CLOSE SHOT - SEIGFRIED AND STEINMUHL

Steinmuhl loosen the Bosun's chair control rope and
together he and Seigfried prepare to pay it out.

98   CLOSE SHOT - MILIZA AND EDELMANN

Miliza, deeply concerned, turns impulsively to Edelmann.

                         MILIZA
            Be careful...

Edelmann nods assuringly and waves his lantern to --

99   SEIGFRIED AND STEINMUHL

-- who start pulling the rope which will carry the Bosun's
chair out over the Hole.

100   MED. FULL SHOT - DEVIL'S HOLE

The seat travels out on the supporting rope until Edelmann
is carried to its center point...

101   INT. DEVIL'S HOLE - CLOSE SHOT - EDELMANN

-- swinging free in space a few feet under the supporting
rope. The b.g. shows only the sheer, smooth side of the
caldron. Edelmann signals again with his lantern. --

102   EXT. NEAR DEVIL'S HOLE - CLOSE SHOT - SEIGFRIED AND
      STEINMUHL

They stop pulling the hauling line and allow the lowering
rope to slip around the snubbing tree.

103   INT. CLOSE SHOT - BRINK OF DEVIL'S HOLE

-- ANGLING UPWARD on Miliza as she stands there, ready to
signal Seigfried and Steinmuhl when to stop.

104   INT. DEVIL'S HOLE - CLOSE SHOT - EDELMANN

-- as the CAMERA DESCENDS with him.

105   EXT. CLOSE SHOT - MILIZA - ON BRINK

She is looking suspensefully downward.

106   INT. BOTTOM OF DEVIL'S HOLE - FULL SHOT

-- ANGLING across the churning waves as Edelmann comes
into view. When he is a few feet from the water, he lets
go the right hand bail and signals upward, by waving his
lantern --

107   EXT. MED. SHOT - MILIZA - ON BRINK

As Miliza signals, Seigfried and Steinmuhl tie the lowering rope around the snubbing tree and join her.

108   INT. DEVIL'S HOLE - MED. SHOT

Edelmann, two or three feet above the water, climbs to a
standing position in the seat. Holding the rope with
both hands, he "pumps" the seat so that it begins to
swing...

109   EXT. BRINK OF DEVIL'S HOLE - MED. CLOSE SHOT

-- ANGLING UPWARD on Miliza, Seigfried and Steinmuhl as
they watch...

110   INT. BOTTOM OF DEVIL'S HOLE - FULL SHOT

-- ANGLING toward the cave's opening. As Edelmann swings
to and fro in a constantly increasing arc, the distance
between him and a narrow ledge becomes shorter and shorter
until finally, when he is directly above it, he lets the
rope slide through his hands and drops the two or three
feet between him and the rocks...

111   MED. CLOSE SHOT - MOUTH OF CAVE

Edelmann lands on the narrow shelf...

112   BRINK OF DEVIL'S HOLE - MED. CLOSE SHOT

-- ANGLING UPWARD on Seigfried, Miliza and Steinmuhl.
All react as they see that Edelmann is safe.

113   BOTTOM OF DEVIL'S HOLE - ANGLING INTO CAVE

Tying the rope of the seat around a jutting rock, Edelmann
turns toward the cavern's entrance...

114   EXT BRINK OF DEVIL'S HOLE - CLOSE SHOT - MILIZA

Seeing that Edelmann is starting to enter the cavern, she
looks off toward ---

115   MED. LONG SHOT - TOWARD EDELMANN'S CASTLE

The moon is closer to the horizon than before...

116   CLOSE SHOT - MILIZA

Concerned, she looks down into the Devil's Hole.

117   INT. CAVE - ANGLING INTO DEVIL'S HOLE

As Edelmann makes his way into the cave, the CAMERA PULLS
BACK with him until he leaves the ledge and steps onto
the cavern's floor, a beach-like deposit of sand, touched
at times by the lapping waves. Here, Edelmann stops,
reacting to --

118   CLOSE SHOT - FLOOR OF CAVE

There are several footprints in the damp sand.

119   CLOSE SHOT - EDELMANN

Reacting to this evidence that Talbot is alive, Edelmann
moves on to a point where the floor is dry. Here, the
footprints disappear -- in a direction which indicates
that Talbot must have crossed the room toward an opening
farther on.

120   MED. FULL SHOT

Edelmann starts toward the opening, but pauses suddenly
as he reacts to something he hears o.s. -- a snarl of
fury as the Wolfman steps through the opening into the
full light of Edelmann's lantern...

121   CLOSE SHOT - TALBOT

He starts forward savagely...

122   MED. SHOT

Edelmann, retreating slowly before Talbot's approach
trips over a stone. As he loses his balance the Wolfman
leaps forward, the force of his onslaught carrying him
and his intended victim to the floor.

CONTINUED

cm

122   CONTINUED

        Edelmann's lantern rolls into a shallow crevice, from
        which it lights the scene weirdly as his fingers grope
        for and find the throat of his opponent, managing by
        force of sheer desperation to hold Talbot far enough
        away to prevent his hairy fingers from closing around
        his throat...

123   EXT. MED. LONG SHOT - TOWARD EDELMANN'S CASTLE

        The moon is beginning to sink below the horizon...

124   INT. CAVE - CLOSE SHOT - TALBOT AND EDELMANN

        Edelmann's arms, holding Talbot away from him, bend slowly
        under his opponent's greater strength until at last, as
        they give way entirely, the Wolfman's fingers close about
        his throat...

125   EXT. MED. LONG SHOT - TOWARD EDELMANN'S CASTLE

        The moon disappears below the horizon...

126   INT. CAVE - MED. CLOSE SHOT - TALBOT AND EDELMANN

        --ANGLING UPWARD over Edelmann so that the Wolfman's
        face is CLOSEUP. As the seizure begins to leave him,
        his grip on Edelmann's throat relaxes. At the same time,
        the CAMERA MOVES CLOSER AND CLOSER during a series of
        fast OVERLAPS in which the hairy growth disappears from
        Talbot's face simultaneously with the return of sanity
        into his eyes, sanity which holds him horrified as he
        stares down at --

127   EDELMANN

        -- who is recovering quickly and is looking up at --

128   TALBOT

        As the final stages of the transition bring normalcy into
        his eyes, Talbot springs to his feet and pulls Edelmann
        up furiously with him.

                        TALBOT
                Why did you follow me down here!

                                        CONTINUED

                              EDELMANN
                         (recovering)
                    To help you...

                              TALBOT
                    You've only dragged me back to a life
                    of misery and despair!
                              (burying his face
                              between his hands)
                    I wanted to die!

                              EDELMANN
                    But instead, you will live ---
                    because in the divine working of
                    his ways, God has led you to the
                    thing which makes help possible...
                              (gripping Talbot's
                              arms)
                    Look about you!
                              (as Talbot uncovers his
                              face)
                    The temperature and humidity down
                    here are ideal for growing the
                    spore producing plants -- and
                    before the next full moon, we
                    should have more than enough to
                    help you!

                              TALBOT
                         (buoyed by hope)
                    You -- you believe that you can?

                              EDELMANN
                    Yes, my boy, yes! But, you must
                    do your part! You must want
                    to live!

                              TALBOT
                         (closing his
                         eyes)
                    I do!

Edelmann grips his arm for a moment of understanding --
then picks up the lantern. As they move to retrace their
steps toward the entrance, both stop suddenly, frozen by
astonishment as the CAMERA ANGLES AWAY and MOVES toward
a roughly circular outlet, about four feet in diameter.
As Edelmann and Talbot (behind the Camera) come closer,
the stronger light shows that a lava-like flow of mud is
moving slowly out of the opening to the floor of the
cavern, terminating at a point where occasional inrolling
waves wash away the mud as fast as it flows in. Near the
edge of the mud is a skeleton -- and in the mud is the
apparently lifeless form of FRANKENSTEIN'S MONSTER. Its
heavy eyelids are closed; its hands reach upward, as though
to seek something to which they can cling.

                                        CONTINUED

128   CONTINUED - 2

                    TALBOT
                (almost inaudibly)
        The Frankenstein Monster...

                    EDELMANN
        And that must be the skeleton of
        Doctor Neimann, who revitalized
        him years ago. When the villagers
        drove them into the marsh, they
        went down in the quicksand --

129   THE MONSTER - CLOSE SHOT

    His fingers move slightly as:

                    EDELMANN'S VOICE
                    (continues)
        -- and mud, which after all these
        years has brought him here ...

130   CLOSE SHOT - EDELMANN AND TALBOT

                    TALBOT
        He's still alive..!

                    EDELMANN
        Frankenstein's creation is man's
        challenge --

131   CLOSE SHOT - MONSTER

    Edelmann bends over into the picture.

                    EDELMANN
        -- to the laws of life and death...
        He will live forever ...

    Trying to make Edelmann understand that he has been heard
    the monster attempts to open his scale-like eyelids. Plac-
    ing the lantern on the ground, Edelmann seizes one of the
    monster's hands and bends its fingers to and fro, watching
    with intense interest as the numbed fingers straighten out
    slowly again.

                    TALBOT'S VOICE
        Doctor! Doctor Edelmann!..

    Reacting to the excitement evident in Talbot's voice,
    Edelmann picks up the lantern and crosses in a PAN SHOT
    toward the opening from which Talbot appeared as the
    Wolfman.

cm

132   CASTLE DUNGEON (TOWER SET) - MED. CLOSE

       -- at the entrance from cave. As Edelmann enters, the
       CAMERA SWINGS AROUND with him, the CHANGING ANGLE REVEAL-
       ING the ancient castle's dungeon. Several disintegrating
       instruments of torture are in evidence, and in the walls
       are imbedded bolts to which are fastened rusted chains with
       leg and wrist bands at their ends. Talbot is standing at
       the foot of the stairway as Edelmann hurries toward him.

133   MED. CLOSE - FOOT OF STAIRS

       Talbot starts excitedly up the stairs as Edelmann enters.

                         TALBOT
                  This must be the way out of here,
                  into the castle..!

                         EDELMANN
                  Its history mentions a torture
                  chamber -- but its entrance was
                  sealed up years ago and the record
                  of its location destroyed...

       He is following Talbot up the stairs as the scene -

                                             DISSOLVES TO

134   INT. SURGERY, LABORATORY - NIGHT - CLOSE SHOT - MONSTER

       (NOTE: In one of the walls there is now an irregular
       opening in the masonry -- the sealed archway through which
       Edelmann and Talbot broke through from the tunnel leading
       downward to the torture chamber.)

       Open on a DOWNWARD ANGLE which shows only the upper third
       of the monster's body. Two flexible cables extend upward
       out of scene from the electrodes in his neck. Offscene is
       heard the sound of the generator, the whirr of which is
       increasing to a whine. Suddenly, there is an o.s. crackle
       from the spark gap of the high-frequency apparatus. Sim-
       ultaneously, tree-like branches of current discharge
       between the neck electrodes and the terminations of the
       cables. As the energizing current begins to take effect,
       the muscles of the monster's face twitch slightly.

       During this, the CAMERA PULLS BACK, showing Edelmann, Nina
       and Talbot standing beside the table on which the monster
       lies strapped. Nina and Talbot exchange disturbed glances
       as Edelmann increases the voltage. There is no fanaticism
       in his manner; rather his attitude is that of a scientist
       whose interest has become deeply aroused.

                                             CONTINUED

                    EDELMANN
        The heart which Frankenstein gave
        him never died... The spark of
        life is there, waiting to be
        revived...

                    TALBOT .
        Doctor Edelmann... This thing
        destroyed Frankenstein -- It's
        brought death to all who tried to
        follow in his footsteps.....

                    EDELMANN
        Is this poor creature responsible
        for what he is...?

                    TALBOT
        It's a thing of violence -- for
        whom death would be merciful
        release...

                    EDELMANN
        Is man to sit in judgment over
        life and death...?

                    NINA
        The evil he creates, he can also
        destroy...

                    EDELMANN
        That would be murder ...
                (he looks down at
                the monster)
        This helpless body is man's
        responsibility...

                    NINA
        Man's first responsibility is to
        man..... To bring him back would
        unleash worse than murder upon
        humanity...

                    EDELMANN
        Don't worry, Nina...Frankenstein's
        monster will never wreak havoc
        again...

        He turns to the instrument panel and, while Talbot and
        Nina watch, opens the control switches. The high-fre-
        quency effects subside as the scene -

                                    DISSOLVES INTO

"DESTINY" - Changes 9/20/45

135   INT. ENTRANCE HALL - <u>NIGHT</u> - M'D. SHOT

PIANO MUSIC, the soft melodic strains of Beethoven's
Moonlight Sonata, is heard o.s. as Dracula enters
through the open doors. He puts his hat and cape on
a table, and then, in a MOVING SHOT, enters the Great
Hall. There, seated at the piano, is Miliza. She is
wearing a simple <u>dinner gown</u>.

136   CLOSE SHOT - MILIZA

Lost in a happy little dream of the music's making, she
is unaware of Dracula's near presence.

137   MED. CLOSE SHOT - REVERSE ANGLE

-- on Dracula as he looks off toward Miliza, smiling as
would a connoisseur who approves of the music he is hearing, but more particularly of the person who is playing
it. As he leaves the reception hall, the CAMERA FOLLOWS
him until the CHANGING ANGLE brings Miliza into view
again.

138   MED. CLOSE SHOT - MILIZA

Becoming suddenly conscious of Dracula's presence, she
looks up with a startled little laugh and stops playing
as he enters.
                        MILIZA
            Why Baron! I didn't hear you...

                        DRACULA
            Please go on...

                        MILIZA
                    (resumes playing)
            You like it?

                        DRACULA
            It breathes the spirit of the night...
                    (after a pause)
            They played it the evening we met,
            at the concert...

                        MILIZA
                    (smiling)
            I'd forgotten it, until I saw you
            again...

                                        CONTINUED

bv

138   CONTINUED

                                DRACULA
                 Perhaps I wanted you to remember...

Miliza, pleased, continues playing for a moment during
which both remain silent.

139   CLOSE SHOT - DRACULA

As he looks off at Miliza, his smile fades and into his
eyes comes the fixed gaze of one who is concentrating
his will.

140   CLOSE SHOT - MILIZA

Miliza's expression takes on the dreamy quality of a person
looking into distant space. Simultaneously, she modulates
the harmony of the sonata into a strange, almost discordant
minor, a pagan, musical distortion which is no longer
peaceful or beautiful. During this, the CAMERA PULLS BACK
to include Dracula.

                                MILIZA
                 I've never heard this music --
                 yet I'm playing it...

                                DRACULA
                 You're creating it -- from what
                 you hear in my mind...

The strange music makes Miliza shudder.

                                MILIZA
                 It frightens me...

                                DRACULA
                 It's beautiful... It's the music
                 of the world from which I come...

                                MILIZA
                 It makes me see strange things --
                 people who are dead -- and who are
                 yet alive...

                                DRACULA
                 Mine is a world without material
                 needs...

                                MILIZA
                 It seems to call me -- but I am
                 afraid...

CONTINUED

                              DRACULA
                    Fear will pass as the music becomes
                    fixed in your mind... It will make
                    you long to be there...

Under the stimulus of these commands, Miliza plays the
music with increasing abandon. As the minors become more
chilling in their weird harmony, the rebellion buried in
her subconscious mind asserts itself until, playing with
one hand only, she raises the other to her neck and finds
the chain of the Crucifix concealed beneath her dress.

As she brings the Cross into view, Dracula averts his
gaze. In that instant, during which the spell is broken,
Miliza drops the Cross back into her bodice and, while
Dracula's face is still turned from her, segues the music
into the final bars of the true melody and, at its conclusion, stands to her feet.

Dracula, turning to her now, attempts to recover control.

                              DRACULA
                    Play the music again...

Miliza, brushing her hand in front of her eyes as would
a person who is trying to remember some forgotten thing,
starts away from the piano.

                              MILIZA
                    There's something -- Doctor
                    Edelmann - told me -- I must
                    do...

As she walks across the room, Dracula follows her into --

141   EDELMANN'S STUDY

          --where, still in the manner of a person who is dreaming
          and is yet awake, Miliza comes down to Edelmann's desk and
          picks up a previously prepared hypodermic from a metal
          tray, turning then to Dracula who, rolling up his coat
          sleeve, catches her eyes with an intent gaze as he tries
          to recapture his lost control over her.

                              DRACULA
                    Listen... To the music...

          The music is heard faintly, a chilling reprise of the pagan
          theme.

                              DRACULA
                    It is in your mind... You are
                    hearing it... Repeating...
                    Repeating...

142   CLOSE SHOT - MILIZA

The dazed look in her eyes gives way to a dreamy, far-
away smile as the music becomes louder...

143   CLOSE SHOT - DRACULA AND MILIZA

Miliza drops the hypodermic unheeded to the floor.

                    DRACULA
          My will is your will...

                    MILIZA
                 (repeating)
          My will is your will...

                    DRACULA
          My world is waiting for you...
          Forsake the Cross, so that you
          may join me there...

Miliza's hand steals slowly upward to the golden chain,
but again her subconscious rebels.

                    MILIZA
          I'm afraid...

The sound of a doorknob turning tells Dracula that someone's entrance into the room is imminent. The MUSIC
FADES as he makes a movement of his hand in front of
Miliza's eyes. To Edelmann, as he enters the room, the
scene presents every appearance of normalcy -- Dracula,
starting to roll down his sleeve as though just having had
his treatment and Miliza, standing nearby in the manner of
having just administered it.

                    EDELMANN
          Thank you, Miliza -- that will
          be all...

Edelmann, oblivious to Miliza's air of abstraction as she
exits, glances at a still limp picture he has evidently
just developed.

                    EDELMANN
          I feel that we're making progress,
          Baron...
                 (exhibiting
                 picture)
          -- but this photomicrograph of
          your blood reveals an odd condition
          -- one which I can't account for
          as yet.

                                        CONTINUED

Dracula takes the photograph, apparently concerned.

                    DRACULA
          What is it, Doctor...?

                    EDELMANN
               (frowning)
          A different species of anti-bodies
          has appeared...

                   ·DRACULA
               (dissembling)
          Why worry, as long as the treat-
          ments are proving successful...?

As he drops the photograph onto the desk and starts toward
the Great Hall exit, Edelmann joins him. The CAMERA
FOLLOWS them to the door.

                    EDELMANN
          When a Doctor effects a cure, he
          likes to know how he did it...

Dracula is starting to open the door.

                    DRACULA
               (smiling)
          Which is of little concern to the
          patient -- as long as he's being
          cured...
               (ready to exit)
          Day after tomorrow...?

                    EDELMANN
          At the usual time.

                    DRACULA
               (warmly)
          Then good night, Doctor.

He exits, closing the door behind him as the scene -

                                        DISSOLVES INTO

144   INT. EDELMANN'S BEDROOM - NIGHT - VERY CLOSE SHOT -
        EDELMANN'S HANDS

        -- holding a book. Its embossed Morocco cover carries
        the title:

                    The Life and Memoirs
                          of
                 Doctor Heinrich Frankenstein

-- from which the CAMERA IS PULLING BACK into a CLOSE
SHOT of Edelmann, seated in a large chair. He wears a
smoking jacket and his feet are outstretched on a hassock.
Bartholomew is purring contentedly in his lap. The top of
the table beside which Edelmann sits is a disorderly lit-
ter of opened books and medical journals, among which a
desk clock is almost buried. The hour is about 3:30...

Edelmann has pulled the shaded reading lamp close to the
edge of the table, so that its light falls upon the pages
of the book and reflects upward into his face. Pausing
in his reading, he lays the book aside and picks up one
of his nearby pipes. Lighting it, he resumes his reading,
puffing away and stroking Bartholomew's back as the scene-

                                    DISSOLVES INTO

145   INT. CASTLE DUNGEON - NIGHT - MED. SHOT

Lamps have been installed. Their wavering flames light
the place with a weird effect. Numerous hothouse "flats"
are scattered about and in them the grotesquely shaped
plants are growing in profusion. On the wall behind a
large table where Nina and Miliza are at work, several
shelves have been constructed. On these are fifty or
more large culture flasks lying side by side, each with
a tuft of cotton in its sloping mouth.

Nina is using a long, spoon-shaped horn spatula to remove
the mold from one of the flasks, sliding the wrinkled pad
into a wide-mouthed beaker. At the conclusion of the
operation, Miliza takes the flask from her and pours some
broth into it from a kettle which is being kept warm on a
small oil burner. During this, Nina takes another flask
from the shelf so that by the time Miliza has returned
hers to its proper place, they are ready to repeat the
routine.

Miliza, whose subconscious is still responsive to Dracula's
influence, wears a manner of deep abstraction. Nina, now
on her way to the shelves, glances at her.

                         NINA
           You're worn out...

Miliza appears not to have heard her. Nina, returning to
the table, pauses for an instant of concern.

                         NINA
           Why don't you get some rest...?

                                    CONTINUED

145   CONTINUED

Miliza looks up slowly. When she speaks, it is as though
she had to grope for her words.

                    MILIZA
          I'm...all...right...

                    NINA
          I know who you're thinking of and
          hoping that we'll be ready in time--
          but the strain is too much for you...
          Go to bed, please Miliza.
               (assuringly)
          I'll finish things down here.

                    MILIZA
               (dazedly)
          I...I think...I will...

146   CLOSE SHOT - MILIZA

She stares absently at the flask in her hand, then becomes
suddenly alert, in the manner of a person listening.
Timed with this, there comes a vibrantly distorted reprise
of the pagan music. Heeding its call, Miliza leaves the
table in a MOVING SHOT which shows her progress toward the
stairs. As she starts slowly up them, the music becomes
louder...

146-A   MED. CLOSE SHOT - NINA - AT TABLE

Engaged in finishing her part of the last routine, she is
far too intent on what she is doing to notice --

146-B   MED. CLOSE SHOT - MILIZA - ON STAIRS

She is moving slowly up to them, as would a person in a
dream.

146-C   MED. CLOSE SHOT - NINA

Concluding the exacting task of fishing a mold pad through
the mouth of the culture flask, she turns to look off
toward --

146-D   CLOSE SHOT - MILIZA - ON STAIRS

She is perilously near the edge of the unprotected stairs
as she stops for an instant, swaying.

146-E   CLOSE SHOT - NINA

NINA
(alarmed)
Miliza! Are you all right!

146-F   CLOSE SHOT - MILIZA

Nina's voice apparently registers in Miliza's subconscious mind, but only to the extent that she continues up the stairs, still oblivious of the fact that she is only a few inches from their edge.

147   MED. CLOSE SHOT - NINA

NINA
Miliza! Be careful!

Receiving no answer, Nina hastens to complete the final part of the routine, then leaves the table in a PAN SHOT which brings the stairs into view. Miliza is not in sight. Nina, deeply disturbed, is hurrying across the room as the scene

WIPES INTO

148   GREAT HALL - MED. SHOT

-- where Dracula, obviously concentrating his will to bring Miliza to him, stands waiting near one of the open French windows. Sensing her near presence, he looks off toward --

149   THE OPPOSITE SIDE OF THE ROOM

Miliza, still in her trance-like state, is entering from the semi-dark hallway.

150   MED. CLOSE SHOT - DRACULA

He takes a few steps away from the window, his CHANGING POSITION bringing him to a point where the large pier-glass, positioned diagonally across that corner of the room, is directly behind him. HOLD on Dracula long enough to deliver the full impact of the revelation that the mirror does not reflect his image.

151   CLOSE SHOT - MILIZA

The CAMERA IS PANNING with her as she crosses the room.

152   HALLWAY - MED. SHOT

Nina is hurrying toward f.g....

153   GREAT HALL - MED. CLOSE SHOT - DRACULA

THE ANGLE is still toward the pier-glass so that as
Miliza enters, her reflection, but not Dracula's, is
seen in the mirror. Dracula takes a step forward, to
meet her...

154   OPPOSITE SIDE OF ROOM - MED. SHOT - INTO HALL

-- as Nina appears, Startled by what she sees, she stops
while still within the semi-darkness.

155   MED. CLOSE SHOT - DRACULA AND MILIZA

As he turns her toward the French window, he moves a light
chair out of their way. In the scene as reflected in the
mirror, the chair moves apparently of its own accord --
pointing up the fact that only its and Miliza's images
are visible...

156   CLOSE SHOT - NINA

Wondering if her eyes are deluding her, Nina catches her
breath and stares o.s. toward --

157   DRACULA AND MILIZA

Dracula is leading her through the French window onto the
garden terrace...

158   MED. CLOSE SHOT - NINA

Mystified and frightened, she runs toward the French window through which Dracula and Miliza made their exit...

159   MED. CLOSE SHOT - FRENCH WINDOW

-- as Nina enters and looks out into --.

160   EXT. GARDEN - MED. SHOT - FROM NINA'S ANGLE

Dracula and Miliza are walking toward one of the trees
which is a short distance from the stairway that leads
up to Miliza's room.

161   INT. GREAT HALL - CLOSE SHOT - NINA

Choking a gasp of fear, Nina turns from the window in a
PAN SHOT which shows her running up the stairway...

162   EXT. GARDEN - MED. CLOSE SHOT - DRACULA AND MILIZA

-- beneath a tree in an ANGLE which establishes the stairway in the b.g. Miliza's gaze is fixed in space as she
stands there with Dracula's eyes upon her...

163   INT. UPPER HALLWAY - MED. SHOT

Nina, breathless from her run up the stairs, comes down
hall and pauses at door of Edelmann's bedroom. She knocks
lightly and reaches for the knob.

                    NINA
             Doctor Edelmann!...

164   INT. EDELMANN'S BEDROOM - MED. CLOSE SHOT - NEAR TABLE

Bartholomew is asleep in Edelmann's lap. Edelmann, still
absorbed in the Memoirs of Frankenstein, is turning to
look toward the door as Nina enters. She is agitated,
flurried to the point of incoherence.

                    EDELMANN
          Yes, Nina...?

                    NINA
          Baron Latos --

                    EDELMANN
                 (reacting to
                  her manner)
          What about him?

                    NINA
          He -- he left here -- early this
          evening -- didn't he?

Edelmann drops Bartholomew from his lap and rises.

                    EDELMANN
          At about half-past eight... Why?

                    NINA
          I -- I...

                    EDELMANN
                 (sharply)
          What is it? Speak up!

                                        CONTINUED

164   CONTINUED

                          NINA
               I just saw him... downstairs...
               Miliza met him... they went --
               into the garden...

        Edelmann moves quickly in a PAN SHOT to -

165   THE WINDOW

        -- where, as Nina enters behind him, he draws the drapes
        partially aside and looks down into --

166   EXT. GARDEN - MED. DOWNWARD ANGLE

        -- as seen by Edelmann. Dracula is talking to Miliza,
        but they are too far away for his voice to be heard.

167   INT. EDELMANN'S BEDROOM - CLOSE SHOT - AT WINDOW

        Nina, having recovered from the initial shock of her
        experience, seeks now to justify her fears by attributing
        them to her imagination, an hallucination induced by
        weariness.

                          NINA
               Miliza and I were working... She
               was awfully tired... She seemed
               like a person in a trance...

                          EDELMANN
                     (facing her quickly)
               In a trance!?

                          NINA
               She left me without saying a word,
               I -- I followed her... She met
               Baron Latos in the Hall
                     (an hysterical
                     little laugh)
               -- and when he walked in front of
               the mirror -- I couldn't see his
               reflection... I -- I imagined that
               -- didn't I?

        Edelmann, as though reluctant to tell her the truth, hesi-
        tates a moment. Nina, attributing his silence to a desire
        not to hurt her, stares at him with returning fear.

                          NINA
                     (almost pleading)
               Didn't I...?

                                              CONTINUED

167   CONTINUED

                        EDELMANN
              No, Nina... Baron Latos shows no
              reflection...

                        NINA
              Then. -- then he's --

She stops with a stifled gasp. Edelmann nods.

                        EDELMANN
              Count Dracula...
                        (as Nina stares
                        at him, stunned)
              In trying to help him, I've
              endangered the lives of all
              of you.

                        NINA
              Knowing who he .was -- you brought
              him here...?

168   INT. EDELMANN'S BEDROOM - CLOSE SHOT - EDELMANN AND NINA

                        EDELMANN
              I've been made a blind and foolish
              dupe, Nina

As he moves with determination toward the door, Nina
follows.

169   INT. UPPER HALLWAY - MED. SHOT - BEDROOM DOOR

As Edelmann and Nina come through, the CAMERA MOVES AHEAD
of them down the hall. During this:

                        EDELMANN
                        (continues)
              -- and must try now to stop him
              before it's too late...

                        NINA
                        (gasping)
              What are you going to do?

                        EDELMANN
              Hold him in check until dawn, if
              I can... Prepare for a transfu-
              sion, at once.

                        NINA
                        (alarmed)
              You can't give another one, so
              soon!.

                                        CONTINUED

During this, the CAMERA HAS SWUNG OFF to one side so that the CHANGING ANGLE shows the stairway which leads to the floor below.

> EDELMANN
> Do as I tell you... And if any-
> thing happens to me, go to the
> armor room in the basement and
> burn what you find there...

They disappear down the stairway...

170   EXT. GARDEN - MED. CLOSE SHOT - MILIZA AND DRACULA

There is a rapt expression upon Miliza's face as Dracula's words hold her spellbound.

> DRACULA
> The music is bringing my world
> closer... closer... closer...
> You're seeing it again... As I
> will you to see it... A world of
> beauty... Of endless time... Of
> eternal love...

> MILIZA
> (enthralled)
> Of eternal love...

> DRACULA
> You long to be there...

> MILIZA
> I long to be there...

> DRACULA
> With me...

> MILIZA
> With you...

> DRACULA
> Then forsake the Cross, so that
> you may join me...

As Miliza's subconscious rebellion succumbs, she draws the Crucifix from her bodice and, while Dracula shields his eyes momentarily from sight of it, drops it to the ground. At the same instant, a flood of light falls suddenly upon them from --

171   THE GREAT HALL - LONG SHOT - FROM THE GARDEN

Edelmann, within the room, has obviously just turned on
the lights and is coming across the room toward the
terrace window.

172   EXT. GARDEN - CLOSE SHOT - DRACULA AND MILIZA

Reacting to Edelmann's unexpected appearance, Dracula
hesitates, then turns quickly to Miliza.

                    DRACULA
          Go to your room... Come to me
          when you hear the music again.

Miliza starts toward the stairway. Dracula, dissembling,
exits toward --

173   THE TERRACE - MED. CLOSE PAN SHOT

As Edelmann starts across the garden with the well-acted
excitement of someone who has just made an important
discovery, he looks off and reacts to --

174   MILIZA - MED. CLOSE SHOT

She is ascending the stairs slowly...

175   CLOSE FOREGROUND SHOT - EDELMANN AND DRACULA - ANGLING
        TOWARD STAIRS

Edelmann joining Dracula, is apparently oblivious to
Miliza, who continues up the stairs and enters her bedroom... Dracula, on guard, watches Edelmann closely.

                    EDELMANN
          I've been looking for you, Baron...!
                    (excitedly)
          You remember that I was puzzled
          tonight -- by the new anti-bodies...?
          I know now where they came from!
          They're from my blood! They must
          be the ones that're helping you --
          and to check the theory I'm going
          to give you another transfusion...

                    DRACULA
          Now, Doctor...?

                    EDELMANN
          Immediately...! If this is the
          answer, we must see, we must see!

                                        CONTINUED

176   CONTINUED

He takes Dracula's arm and starts across the garden in a
PAN SHOT toward the surgery, within which lights are
coming in as the scene --

                                        DISSOLVES TO

176   INT. LABORATORY, SURGERY - MED. SHOT - ANGLING DOWNWARD

-- from PARALLEL over Nina's back so that her body conceals her operation of the transfusion apparatus on the
stand between the tables on which Edelmann and Dracula
lie... Dracula has his gaze fixed in space. Edelmann
is tense, hopeful that his subterfuge will keep Dracula
here until after dawn...

177   CLOSE SHOT - NINA

-- in an UPWARD ANGLE. She is trying to hide her real
emotions, but fear reflects in her eyes as she looks down
at --

178   CLOSE SHOT - DRACULA

-- whose gaze is still fixed in space.

179   CLOSE SHOT - EDELMANN

Weakened by loss of blood, he closes his eyes...

180   CLOSE SHOT - NINA

As she sees Edelmann's condition, she gasps.

                         NINA
              Doctor...!

181   CLOSE SHOT - EDELMANN

Aroused by Nina's voice, he opens his eyes with an effort..

182   CLOSE SHOT - DRACULA

-- in a DOWNWARD ANGLE as he directs his gaze toward --

183   NINA

-- who is momentarily unaware that Dracula's eyes are
fixed upon her while she looks down at --

184   EDELMANN

Unable to resist the lethargy which has taken hold of him,
he closes his eyes...

185   CLOSE SHOT - NINA

Increasing alarm seizes her as she sees that Edelmann has
lost consciousness...

186   CLOSE SHOT - DRACULA

His gaze becomes more compelling as he stares up at --

187   NINA

-- who turns slowly to look down at him. She closes her
eyes -- then, swaying slightly, opens them again to look
at --

188   DRACULA

-- whose image blurs and melts grotesquely as he starts
to sit up...

189   CLOSE SHOT - NINA

The transfusion siphon falls from her hands as she lifts
one of them slowly and brushes it before her eyes...

190   MED. GROUP SHOT

Nina, undistorted, stands swaying before the PROCESS SCENE
in which Dracula and the tables upon which he and Edelmann
lie melt and run together in a surrealistic nightmare.
During this, Dracula rises and stands beside his table,
tearing from his arm the donor tube which now slopes downward to Edelmann's arm. Nina sinks slowly to the floor...

191   CLOSE SHOT - NINA - ON FLOOR

She lies there dazed, but not wholly unconscious.

192   MED. SHOT

        Dracula looks at Edelmann triumphantly for an instant,
        then exits into the garden.

193   CLOSE SHOT - NINA - ON FLOOR

        She regains her faculties and rises in a PAN SHOT beside
        the table on which Edelmann lies.

                              NINA
                         (shaking his
                           shoulder)
                   Doctor! Doctor Edelmann...!

194   EXT. GARDEN - CLOSE PAN SHOT - DRACULA

        He reaches the center of the garden and stands there,
        looking off toward the lighted window of Miliza's room.

195   INT. LABORATORY, SURGERY - MED. CLOSE SHOT

        Nina has one arm under Edelmann's shoulder, supporting
        him in a partially sitting position while with her other
        hand, she helps him hold a glass from which he is drinking
        a stimulant.

196   EXT. GARDEN - CLOSE PAN SHOT - DRACULA

        He moves a few paces forward, keeping his gaze concen-
        trated in the direction of Miliza's room.

197   INT. LABORATORY, SURGERY - MED. CLOSE SHOT

        Edelmann, weak from loss of blood, slips off the table
        and stands there swaying, supported by Nina.

198   EXT. GARDEN - CLOSE SHOT - DRACULA

        The pagan music comes in faintly as Dracula concentrates
        his gaze toward Miliza's room.

199   INT. MILIZA'S BEDROOM - CLOSE SHOT - MILIZA

        -- lying on the chaise lounge. She stirs slightly and
        opens her eyes as the music becomes louder.

200   INT. LABORATORY, SURGERY - MED. CLOSE PAN SHOT

Nina is only a step or so behind Edelmann as he staggers
across toward the terrace window.

201   EXT. GARDEN - CLOSE SHOT - DRACULA

He looks off toward the garden wall. Realizing that the
dawn is imminent, he raises his arms so that the folds of
his opera cape spread out like the wings of a monstrous
bird... as a DISSOLVE transmutes him into a Gargantuan
bat which circles above the garden.

202   INT. EDELMANN'S STUDY - MED. CLOSE

Edelmann and Nina ENTER. She stifles a gasp as they react
to --

203   MED. SHOT THRU WINDOW

The giant bat wings its way past window and continues
toward Miliza's room.

204   CLOSE SHOT - EDELMANN AND NINA

Nina, stifling a scream of horror, runs out towards Larry's
room.

205   INT. EDELMANN'S STUDY - LONGER SHOT

Edelmann's actions are those of a man who is driving him-
self into physical exertion by sheer force of his will.
He staggers to the fireplace, snatches a carved walnut
Cross from above the mantel and then exits into --

206   EXT. GARDEN TERRACE - MED. FULL SHOT

Edelmann enters from his study and starts in an unsteady
run across the garden toward the balcony stairs as the
bat flies through the window into Miliza's room.

207   INT. BEDROOM HALLWAY - CLOSE SHOT - AT DOOR

as Nina runs breathlessly in and knocks frantically.

                     NINA
              Mr. Talbot! Mr. Talbot..!

208   INT. MILIZA'S BEDROOM - MED. FULL SHOT

Miliza is still lying upon the chaise lounge as the bat
circles above her and then dematerializes in a TRICK
EFFECT which transmutes him into Dracula again...

209   EXT. GARDEN - MED. SHOT - TOWARD BALCONY STAIRS

The CAMERA ANGLES with Edelmann as he lunges into the
foot of the stairs, clutching the iron rail for support
as he pauses.

210   INT. MILIZA'S BEDROOM - MED. SHOT

A sensuous, lustful smile is now upon Miliza's face as
Dracula puts an arm about her and turns her toward the
balcony window...

211   EXT. GARDEN - BALCONY STAIRS - UPWARD ANGLE

The CAMERA ANGLES with Edelmann as he drives himself up
the stairs to the balcony...

212   INT. MILIZA'S BEDROOM - MED. CLOSE SHOT - BALCONY WINDOW

-- as Edelmann appears. All but spent, he has to stop...

213   MED. FULL SHOT

Dracula, with one arm about Miliza, stops suddenly and
shields his eyes with his cape as Edelmann starts across
the room, holding the Crucifix up in front of him. Miliza,
appearing like one in a carnal, wanton dress, closes her
eyes and stands there, swaying... The door behind her and
Dracula opens suddenly...

214   MED. CLOSE SHOT - DOOR

Talbot and Nina enter, out of breath. Nina stops, spellbound by horror as Talbot runs past her into the room.

215   FULL SHOT

As Edelmann comes closer, Dracula evades him blindly and
runs toward the balcony. Edelmann pursues him with the
Crucifix, while Talbot, reaching Miliza just as she
starts to follow Dracula, catches her in his arms and
holds her against her will.

216   EXT. GARDEN - MED. SHOT - ANGLING UP STAIRWAY

        Dracula, fleeing before the Cross, runs down the stairs.
        As Edelmann staggers out onto the balcony, Dracula, now
        in a CLOSE SHOT at the foot of the stairs, looks off
        with increasing terror as he sees -

217   LONG SHOT - TOWARD GARDEN WALL

        As seen by Dracula through a vista among the trees, fan-
        like streamers of light reach upward, edging the morning
        clouds with silver.

218   CLOSE SHOT - DRACULA.

        Shielding his eyes, he flees in a PAN SHOT across the
        garden toward the Great Hall terrace..

219   CLOSE SHOT - EDELMANN - AT FOOT OF BALCONY STAIRS

        The CAMERA PANS with him as he starts across the garden
        in the direction of Dracula's exit.

220   INT. MILIZA'S BEDROOM - MED. SHOT

        Talbot has placed Miliza upon the lounge and is chafing
        her hands. Nina's eyes are filled with dread as she
        looks down at Miliza's apparently lifeless body.

221   INT. BASEMENT ROOM - MED. FULL SHOT

        Daylight is filtering in through the windows as Dracula
        descends the steps and runs in terror toward his coffin.

222   MED. CLOSE - TOP OF STEPS

        Edelmann appears, made breathless by his exertion. The
        CAMERA ANGLES with him as he descends the steps, the
        CHANGING ANGLE bringing Dracula's coffin again into view.

223   MED. CLOSE - DRACULA'S COFFIN

        As Edelmann comes toward f.g., the coffin's lid is descen-
        ding and Dracula's fingers are being withdrawn into the
        interior just as the soft light becomes a shaft of bril-
        liance in the mote-filled air. Edelmann, now beside the
        coffin, debates his course of action for a moment -- then
        makes his decision. Putting the Crucifix in his pocket,
        he pulls Dracula's coffin from its supporting blocks,
        dragging it across the floor until the beam of sunlight
        spreads along its entire length. This done, he raises
        the coffin's lid.

224   FULL DOWNWARD ANGLE - INTO COFFIN

The sun's full glory falls upon Dracula from head to feet.
As the substance of his body dissolves into a skeleton,
the MUSIC CLIMAXES in one last shrieking note which might
well be his death cry.

225   INT. MILIZA'S BEDROOM - GROUP SHOT

As Dracula's death releases Miliza from his control, the
light of sanity returns slowly to her eyes. Recognizing
Talbot, she clings to him with a sob of relief.

                    MILIZA
          Oh, Larry... It was horrible...

Talbot holds her comfortingly in his arms. Nina, smiling,
moves toward the hall door and exits as the scene -

                                        WIPES TO

226   INT. BASEMENT CORRIDOR - MED. CLOSE SHOT - DOOR

Edelmann, entering from the room beyond, is closing and
locking the door as Nina appears. Weak now that the
strength born of his excitement begins to pass, Edelmann
sways unsteadily, but pulls himself together as Nina
reaches him.

                    EDELMANN
          Miliza...?

                    NINA
                 (assuringly)
          She's all right, now...

Edelmann closes his eyes -- a moment of silent, forvent
relief.

                    EDELMANN
                 (almost inaudibly)
          The evil I brought her will never
          live again...

Nina places her hand upon his arm in a gesture of unspoken
understanding. As Edelmann turns away, it appears that
some strange and baffling change has taken place, for as
he walks slowly toward the CAMERA, he is staring unseeingly
into distant space as the scene -

                                        DISSOLVE INTO

227   INT. EDELMANN'S BEDROOM - NIGHT - CLOSE SHOT

        --ANGLING DOWNWARD on Edelmann's walking feet as the
        CAMERA PULLS BACK into a LARGER SHOT. The strange ner-
        vousness which Edelmann experienced that morning appears
        to have taken hold of him more strongly. He stops beside
        his chair, in which Bartholomew lies curled asleep, and
        then as a person will sometimes do, unconsciously inter-
        locks his fingers and twists them to flex their muscles.
        The act of doing this causes him to lower his eyes. With
        a frown which reflects professional curiosity and brings
        him around the chair close to the table, Edelmann holds
        his hands into the cone of light from the lamp. Leaning
        over, and seeing nothing as yet to explain the peculiar
        feeling he has in his fingers, Edelmann massages them for
        a moment, then resumes his restless pacing...

228   CLOSE SHOT - BARTHOLOMEW

        He awakens suddenly, aroused by some strange animal
        instinct as he looks off toward -

229   EDELMANN

        --walking slowly up and down the room in a PAN SHOT. He
        has his hands behind him and is twisting his interlocked
        fingers.

230   CLOSE SHOT - BARTHOLOMEW

        His eyes are gleaming and alert as they now begin to
        follow Edelmann's movements...

231   MED. CLOSE SHOT - TABLE

        Again Edelmann stops at the table and examines his hands,
        reacting with shock as he sees --

232   CLOSE SHOT - EDELMANN'S HANDS

        He separates his fingers, revealing that web-like, mem-
        branous triangles of translucent flesh have begun to grow
        between them.

233   CLOSE SHOT - EDELMANN

        --in an UPWARD ANGLE which shows him staring at his hands
        and at the same time reveals that some subtle metamor-
        phosis is transmuting the gentle character lines of his
        face so that almost imperceptibly his expression is begin-
        nning to take on a harsh, malevolent quality...

234   MED. CLOSE SHOT - AT TABLE

--in an ANGLE which includes Bartholomew in the chair.
His fur is beginning to rise as he keeps his eyes fixed
on Edelmann who now, with a gasp of horror, turns away
from the table, stricken by a sudden and terrifying
thought which hastens his steps toward --

235   THE DRESSER

-- before which he stops, unable to believe what he sees
taking place; first, the physical change which is coming
over his face and second, the fact that the image which
looks back at him from the mirror is already semi-trans-
parent and is becoming more and more so with each passing
second.

236.   CLOSE SHOT - BARTHOLOMEW

He is now standing on the arm of the chair. His back is
arched and his fur is bristling as he keeps his eyes fixed
as though fascinated upon --

237   EDELMANN - IN FRONT OF MIRROR

The part of his consciousness which is his real self,
brings horror into his eyes as his image becomes fainter
and fainter, until it disappears altogether...

238   CLOSE SHOT - BARTHOLOMEW

His lips curl back over his gleaming white teeth as he
stares off toward Edelmann, spitting, and then jumps from
the chair in a PAN SHOT which follows him until he darts
out of the window into the night...

239   MED. SHOT

Stunned by what he has seen in the mirror, Edelmann leaves
the dresser and lurches his way to the table, pausing
there to plunge his outstretched hands into the cone of
light.

240   CLOSE SHOT - EDELMANN'S HANDS

The webs of flesh between the fingers have grown larger;
the fingernails, now elongated slightly, are curved downward, giving his hands a half-human, half-vulture-like
appearance.

cm

241   CLOSE SHOT - EDELMANN

        Shaken to his very soul by the full realization of what
        has taken place, he slumps over the table with a broken
        inarticulate sob choking in his throat. As this first
        reaction passes, the CAMERA MOVES FORWARD SLOWLY, bringing
        his outstretched hands closer and closer into view show-
        ing his taloned fingers clutching and tearing at the
        felt of the table top. Now, as he raises his head, it is
        instantly evident that the thing which seized him at the
        mirror has gained stronger and stronger domination over
        his real self. His character lines have etched evil deeply
        into his face;--his eyes, dilated somewhat, are becoming
        more and more filled with cruel light which would indicate
        that the thoughts running riot in his mind are no longer
        horrifying to him, but rather are giving him pleasure of
        a demoniacal, sadistic nature. During these transitions,
        the CAMERA HAS MOVED STILL CLOSER, so that when Edelmann's
        eyes almost fill the screen, they blur out into a pair of
        swirling, nebula-like maelstroms which merge and -

                                            DISSOLVE INTO

242   A MONTAGE
thru
265   -- composed of the following CUTS, WIPES AND DISSOLVES,
        SCORED to emphasize the remorseless malevolence of the
        phantasmagoria which is taking place in Edelmann's mind.

        A. EDELMANN'S BASEMENT ROOM. Dracula's coffin remains
            as we last saw it, as the ghost-like transparent figure
            of Dracula rises from it. The musical score picks up
            the reprise of the pagan theme so that the highest
            notes can be interpreted as an expression of Dracula's
            triumphant, mocking laughter. As the wraith-like
            figure moves TOWARD CAMERA Dracula raises his arm,
            pointing a scornful finger at the lens. During this
            action a CLOSEUP of the real Dr. Edelmann's face is
            SUPERIMPOSED reacting in horror.

        B. A STORM TORMENTED MOUNTAIN TOP upon whose rain-beaten
            and wind-swept pinnacle stands Edelmann's evil figure
            revealed in chiseled brilliance by flashes of lightning.
            The SCORE INTERPRETS his laughter into the satanic joy
            of a demon defying the laws of God and man as, looking
            down from the eminence, he beckons maniacally to --

        C. THE FRANKENSTEIN MONSTER, drenched by the torrential
            downpour and lashed by lightning as he climbs ponder-
            ously up the muddy slope like some aborted horror
            escaping from Hell.

        D. Edelmann is a figure of fiendish, malignant evil as
            he beckons the monster on and on...

                                            CONTINUED

cm

242
thru
265

CONTINUED

E. STOCK SHOT. The white-crested waves of a BOOMING SURF
surge forward in an engulfing wall of water through
which --

F. -- there appears a SCENE in EDELMANN'S GARDEN. Talbot
and Miliza are walking toward CAMERA. They are a
picture of idyllic happiness.

G. EDELMANN'S FACE blends over the scene. His laughter
is that of a man who has bartered his soul to the devil.

H. THE MONSTER crushes Miliza in his arms.

I. Laughing sadistically, EDELMANN beckons the Monster on.

J. As the MONSTER throws Miliza's lifeless body to the
ground, a blast of lightning envelops him...

K. THE VILLAGE STREET, where men, women and children are
fleeing in terror before him...

L. EDELMANN, laughing crazily, pantomines to the Monster
what he is to do.

M.) FAST CUTS OF EDELMANN urging the Monster on into scenes
N.) in which he hurls the villagers away from him as though
O.) they were matchwood...Over the last of these CUTS --
P.)

Q. A CLOSEUP, showing Edelmann's exultant, evil joy, blends
into --

R. AN ASTRONOMIC PICTURE OF THE STARRY FIRMAMENT, reflected
in a mirroring pool of water in which float myriad surgical instruments in slow motion. A sudden rippling of
the water distorts the scene into --

S. A SURGICAL TABLE on which Nina lies unconscious while
Edelmann bends over her, apparently performing the
operation as the entire scene recedes from the Camera
with the speed of an express train until it becomes
only a point in a swirling vortex which melts into --

T. GARDEN. NINA, dressed in soft enveloping white, is
walking toward Edelmann. Her deformity has been cor-
rected and she now stands erect and strong and smiling
as Edelmann promised her she would.

U. EDELMANN. His dilating eyes are filled with inhuman
cruelty as he starts toward the Camera...

V. NINA, still smiling, is walking toward Edelmann...

CONTINUED

242
thru
265

CONTINUED - 2

W. EDELMANN. His bestial face is coming closer and closer.

X. NINA. Oblivious apparently to the evil in the face of the man she worships, Nina's eyes are shining with gratitude as her blind faith carries her on toward Edelmann. As his hands reach out toward her throat, the MONTAGE is -

DISSOLVING INTO

266   INT. EDELMANN'S BEDROOM - CLOSE SHOT

The CAMERA IS PULLING BACK from a CLOSEUP of Edelmann's eyes, which burn fiercely with an unholy light. Now in the final phase of the transition which has aroused such primal, bestial impulses, he gets to his feet and weaves across the room toward the door, exiting into the hall as the scene -

DISSOLVES INTO

267   INT. SURGERY, LABORATORY - CLOSEUP - MONSTER - ON TABLE

An o.s. CRASH of sparks from the high-frequency apparatus is heard simultaneously with the appearance of electrical discharges between the ends of the cables and the electrodes in the Monster's neck. On this the CAMERA is PULLING BACK into a LARGER SHOT which shows Edelmann, still in the grip of his seizure, looking down at the Monster, turning the voltage control higher and higher as he bends over the table. The Monster's eyelids flutter open. Edelmann, reacting with an inarticulate cackle of maniacal delight, increases the voltage still higher.

268   HALLWAY - CLOSE SHOT - LABORATORY DOOR

Nina is standing there, holding a tray on which is a pot of coffee and some covered dishes. Reacting with worry to the SOUND EFFECTS coming from the laboratory, she hesitates a moment -- then knocks on the door.

                    NINA
          Doctor Edelmann...

269   INT. SURGERY, LABORATORY - CLOSE SHOT - EDELMANN

He apparently doesn't hear Nina's voice. As he increases the voltage again, one of the cables fuses away from its electrode in the Monster's neck. Edelmann, with a snarl, opens the control switch. As the SOUND EFFECTS SUBSIDE, he reacts to -

                              CONTINUED

269   CONTINUED

                              NINA'S VOICE
                    Doctor... I have your supper...

Edelmann whirls toward the door.

                              EDELMANN
                    Go away... Leave me alone...

270   HALLWAY - CLOSE SHOT - NINA

The harsh quality in Edelmann's voice has brought instant
concern into her expression.

                              NINA
                    Doctor! Let me in!

271   SURGERY, LABORATORY - CLOSE SHOT - AT TABLE

                              EDELMANN
                    Go away, I tell you!

Even as he says this, he leaves the table in a PAN SHOT
whose CHANGING ANGLE is from behind him as he moves toward
the door.

272   HALLWAY - CLOSE SHOT - NINA

Thoroughly alarmed, she tries the door. It is locked.

273   SURGERY, LABORATORY - CLOSE SHOT - AT HALL DOOR

The CAMERA IS STILL BEHIND Edelmann as his hand reaches
out toward the key, pausing only when within a few inches
of it.

                              NINA'S VOICE
                            (pleadingly)
                    Doctor! Doctor Edelmann!

Edelmann's hand reaches slowly toward --

274   CLOSE SHOT - KEY IN LOCK

Edelmann's hand comes into view. Seizing the key, he
starts to unlock the door as the CAMERA RECEDES INTO A
LARGER SHOT which is an ANGLE FROM BEHIND him so that
his face is not seen. As he turns the knob, the tense-
ness of his body begins to relax. Simultaneously with
starting to open the door, he straightens up slowly --

275   HALLWAY - MED. CLOSE SHOT - ANGLING TOWARD DOOR

Puzzled, but not frightened, Nina's forehead contracts
in lines of worried concern as the door opens several
inches, stops for two or three seconds -- then continues
opening slowly...

276   CLOSE SHOT - NINA

As she stares straight ahead, her expression of increasing concern might easily be attributable to horror as more
and more light falls upon her through the constantly wid-
ening space of the opening door.

277   REVERSE SHOT - ANGLING OVER NINA TOWARD DOOR

-- through which Edelmann is PICKED UP at the very instant
in which the last trace of his seizure passes and leaves
him the same kindly-spoken doctor whom Nina has always
known, but a man whose expression reflects the tragic
realization of how close he came to having on his hands
the blood of this gentle, trusting girl...

278   NINA - FROM BEHIND EDELMANN

Seeing Edelmann's manner, Nina assumes that it is the
consequence of what he went through that morning.

                          NINA
           You're ill...!

                        EDELMANN
                    (striving for
                    control)
         I -- I'm all right...

                        NINA
                    (assertively)
         After what you went through this
         morning, you need rest...

Edelmann, managing a drawn smile of appreciation, exits
with Nina as the scene -

                               DISSOLVES TO

279   EDELMANN'S BEDROOM - MED. CLOSE - HALL DOOR

Nina is entering from the hall, followed by Edelmann.
Placing the tray upon the table, she fluffs the cushions
of his chair. As Edelmann sinks into it with a tired
sigh and closes his eyes, Nina fills the cup from the
coffee pot and hands it to him.

                               CONTINUED

279   CONTINUED

                              NINA
            This will make you feel better...

Edelmann takes the cup. As he drinks, he manages a smile,
an effort to assure Nina that he is now himself.

280   CLOSE SHOT - NINA

She tries not to show it, but her concern deepens...

281   CLOSE SHOT - EDELMANN

He pauses in his drinking -- a few seconds during which
the determination takes form in his mind that what lies
ahead must be done before the horror returns again and
makes it impossible.

282   CLOSE SHOT - NINA AND EDELMANN

As he finishes drinking, Nina takes the cup from his hand.

                              EDELMANN
            How much of the spore solution
            have we ready...?

                              NINA
            We're making fine progress... Don't
            worry about that, now...

Edelmann's voice is sharp without intentionally being so.

                              EDELMANN
                    (a. he rises)
            Answer me. Is there enough for
            the two operations...?

                              NINA
                    (puzzled)
            No... There won't be, for several
            days...

                              EDELMANN
                    (insistently)
            But we've enough for one?

                              NINA
                    (sensing what is
                    in his mind)
            I... I think so...

                                        CONTINUED

282   CONTINUED

                    EDELMANN
          Then I must operate as soon as
          possible... On you...

Seeing the unspoken question in her eyes, Edelmann quickly
seizes upon her previously spoken line as a cue to explain
the urgency behind his sudden decision.

                    EDELMANN
                 (continues)
          I am ill -- as you said... It's
          impossible to see what the future
          holds...

                    NINA
                 (shocked)
          You mustn't talk like that!

                    EDELMANN
                 (with finality)
          I'll operate tomorrow, Nina.

                    NINA
                 (with equal finality)
          On Mr. Talbot... The moon will be
          full in a few days --
                 (compassionately)
          We can't let him suffer again...

                    EDELMANN
          You've waited a long time...

                    NINA
          A little while longer will make
          no difference....

As she EXITS, the CAMERA MOVES UP CLOSE to Edelmann. He
looks after her, smiling, touched by her unselfish
generosity; but then, as the pagan music of the Dracula
theme is heard very, very faintly, a frown comes over his
face -- a frown of bitterness as he remembers Nina's last
words. Will there be time to help her, too...?

                                   DISSOLVE TO

F;   "DESTINY"- 9/14/45

283   INT. SURGERY, LABORATORY- <u>NIGHT</u>- MED. GROUP SHOT

The CAMERA is ANGLING DOWNWARD from ABOVE a large reflector lamp. Within the cone of light concentrated upon
the operating table on which Talbot lies, stand Miliza,
Edelman and Nina. All wear surgical whites, but no masks,
as this is not the type of operation which requires them.
Edelman is removing his rubber gloves, while Miliza com-
pletes the bandage which swathes Talbot's head. During
this action the CAMERA LOWERS AND DROPS BACK INTO A
NORMAL GROUP SHOT. Edelman turns now to the table and
takes Talbot's pulse while Nina, opposite him, holds her
hand upon Talbot's chest, counting his respiration. During
the period of silence, Miliza looks down at Talbot's mask-
like face.

                         EDELMAN
                    (to Nina)
          Respiration?

                         NINA
          Eighteen...Normal...
                    (there is awe in
                    her voice)
          It's wonderful, Doctor Edelmann...
          What you've done would ordinarily
          mean an operation of the most
          delicate nature. This way, the
          dangers of surgery didn't even
          exist....

Edelmann has pushed back one of Talbot's eyelids to
examine the pupilary dilation.

                         EDELMANN
          Even so, it will be a shock to
          his nervous system...
                    (to Miliza)
          See that he's kept quiet.
          Exertion might undo everything
          I hope we've accomplished.
                    (as he sees the
                    unspoken question
                    in her eyes, his voice
                    becomes sympathetically
                    gentle)
          We'll know in a few days, Miliza...
          All we can do now is hope...

                         MILIZA
                    (almost inaudibly)
          And pray...

284   CLOSE SHOT - EDELMANN

When he speaks, his voice tells clearly that the prayer
he has in mind is not wholly for Talbot.

                         EDELMANN
              Yes, Miliza... and pray...
                   (looking across
                    table)
              Nina... Every minute must be
              devoted now to processing more
              ¯of the spores -- for you...

He turns almost abruptly and is starting to exit as the
scene --

                                        DISSOLVES INTO

35   INT. TALBOT'S BEDROOM - NIGHT - CLOSE SHOT - DOOR

The door opens and Nina enters. She carries a tray, on
which there is a pitcher of milk and a glass. There is
a knowing little smile on her face as she looks o.s.,
then moves into the room in a PAN SHOT which brings
Talbot and Miliza into view. Talbot's head is bandaged
lightly. Miliza is standing beside the wheelchair in
which he sits... Nina puts the tray on the table and
starts to fill the glass.

                         NINA
                   (admonishingly)
              You're a fine nurse, Miliza...
              You know very well Mr. Talbot
              should be asleep by now...

                         TALBOT
              Sleep? -- I'll have a life time
              in which to sleep -- after I know --
              what lies ahead.

                         NINA
              After what Doctor Edelmann has
              done for you -- only happiness
              lies ahead.

                         TALBOT
              I wonder ---

                                        CONTINUED

.285   CONTINUED

He turns his chair sudde   y and wheels it toward the
French window which opens onto the porch. Miliza and
Nina glance at each other for an instant of understanding
-- then Miliza hurries out after him...

286   PORCH OF TALBOT'S ROOM

Miliza follows Talbot out onto the porch. The CAMERA
MOVES UP INTO AN INTIMATE CLOSE SHOT as Talbot propels
his chair to where Miliza, understanding his mood, sits
on the edge of the broad balustrade. There is a moment
of silence, during which both of them look out into the
night.

                    TALBOT
        Miliza...

                    MILIZA
        Yes, Larry...?

287   CLOSE SHOT - TALBOT

Staring moodily beyond them, he turns now and looks up
at her.

                    TALBOT
        Don't think I'm ungrateful... but --

288   CLOSE TWO SHOT

                    TALBOT
                (bitterly)
        -- time after time I've clung to
        the hope that someone might be able
        to help me -- and time after time
        those who've tried, have failed...
                (his voice grows grim)
        If this fails...

289   CLOSE SHOT - MILIZA

Her voice is gentle with understanding.

                    MILIZA
        It won't, Larry! Believe that it
        won't!

                                        CONTINUED

289-A   MED. TWO SHOT

                    TALBOT
          I've tried to - I want to - but
          when I face the nights...

                    MILIZA
          Try to see the night as something
          beautiful.

                    TALBOT
                (looking out into
                 the night)
          -- Until the moon turns it into a
          thing of ugliness and horror...

                    MILIZA
          You'll see it soon as everyone else
          sees it - restful, tranquil and serene...

                    TALBOT
          -- Until that time comes - I'll live a
          thousand hopes and die a thousand deaths.

                    MILIZA
                (impassioned)
          It will never be ugly to you again,
          Larry -- I know it.

Talbot takes her hand and looks into her eyes as if
seeking an answer.

                    TALBOT
          How do you know it?

                    MILIZA
          My heart tells me.

Talbot lowers his head as if he had found the answer in
her eyes, then presses her hand to his cheek.

                    TALBOT
          Then I must know it too -- It means
          so much to me...

                    MILIZA
                (softly)
          -- To both of us...

                              DISSOLVE TO

290   INT. EDELMANN'S BEDROOM - CLOSE SHOT - BARTHOLOMEW

The animal is curled up on the cushion of Edelman's easy
chair, asleep. Its ears prick up suddenly, and, instantly
awake, his eyes focus on and follow the movements of
Edelmann, who is not seen. Now, Bartholomew's hairs begin
to bristle... Spitting fear, he jumps from the arm of the
chair and dashes toward the window in a PAN SHOT.

F:

290   CONTINUED

As he runs out into the night, the CAMERA MOVES TOWARD
THE WINDOW, bringing Edelmann into view as he enters,
tense and taut in every muscle, his manner making it ob-
vious that he is starting toward Bartholomew when the animal fled...As Edelmann stands at the window, his attention
turns in another direction...

291   ANGLING THROUGH WINDOW INTO INTERIOR. CLOSE SHOT-EDELMANN

It is apparent now that the change is imminent, for as
he stands there, looking off, crafty cunning comes into
his eyes...

292   EXT. CASTLE COURT-MED. CLOSE SHOT- AT END OF WAGON

As Seigfried heaves the drum into the body of the wagon,
the CAMERA PANS AWAY AND SWINGS UPWARD to--

293   CLOSE SHOT- TALBOT- ON PORCH

--as he looks off with cursory interest toward---

294   The o.s. noises of the moving wagon are heard as Talbot,
reacting now to another sound, turns his gaze in another
direction...

295   COURT- MED. LONG PAN SHOT

HOLD on Edelmann as he appears from the building and runs
after the wagon until the CHANGING ANGLE brings it into
view.

296   CLOSE SHOT- TALBOT- ON PORCH

He obviously thinks that the procedure is at least an
unusual one as his eyes follow---

297   EDELMANN

--who, overtakes the wagon and pulls himself up into the
body...

298   CLOSE SHOT- TALBOT- ON PORCH

Watching curiously, he leans further over the balustrade
so that he can see----

299   THE COURTWAY- LONG SHOT

--from Talbot's ANGLE, showing Edelmann now in the wagon
as it continues toward the gates....

300   INT. WAGON - ON EDELMANN'S DRIVEWAY - (PROCESS) -
          MED. CLOSE SHOT - SEIGFRIED

          He is humming a folk song, unaware of Edelmann's presence
          in the body of the wagon, behind him.

301   CLOSE SHOT - EDELMANN

          He is crouched beside the oil drum, looking back toward
          the castle. The first evidence of the transition is now
          beginning to manifest itself, a slight change which is
          just noticeable. Assured that he has not been seen, Edel-
          mann turns his eyes toward--

302   THE WAGON SEAT - (PROCESS) - MED. CLOSE SHOT - SEIGFRIED

          He is still humming as Edelmann crawls along the floor of
          the wagon and, holding onto the edge of the seat, pulls
          himself up slowly until he is very close to Seigfried.
          The old man, sensing the presence of someone near him,
          reacts with a start of surprise as he sees Edelmann, who
          is now in the second stage of his transition -- a change
          which is more noticeable to us at the moment than it is to
          Seigfried, to whom Edelmann still appears to be himself.

                              SEIGFRIED
                   Doctor Edelmann...!

          As Edelmann answers the smile on his face carries some-
          what the quality of a leer.

                              EDELMANN
                   Didn't you hear me call to you,
                   Seigfried...?

          He sits on the edge of the seat and starts to swing him-
          self around.

303   CLOSE SHOT - SEIGFRIED - (PROCESS)

                              SEIGFRIED
                       (confused)
                   Why no, sir...

          As he glances off at Edelmann, the old man senses some-
          thing strange in his master's manner, his first feeling
          that something is wrong.

                              SEIGFRIED
                     (continued)
                   I'd have stopped for you, if I had...

bv

304   CLOSE SHOT - EDELMANN (PROCESS)

The third stage in his transition is now in progress, one during which the flexing of his fingers becomes more and more intense...

                    EDELMANN
                 (almost purring)
         I'm certain you would have --
                 (patting Seigfried's
                  shoulder)
         Don't worry about it, Seigfried...

305   CLOSE SHOT - SEIGFRIED - (PROCESS)

Trying to conceal his uneasiness, Seigfried snaps the reins and clucks to the horse.

306   CLOSE SHOT - EDELMANN - (PROCESS)

The fourth stage in the change is bringing a crueler and more sadistic light into his eyes. As he keeps them fixed on Seigfried, his smile becomes a leer and his fingers begin to take on a talon-like quality.

307   CLOSE SHOT - SEIGFRIED - (PROCESS)

Feeling Edelmann's gaze upon him, he glances sidelong out of his eyes, reacting with increasing fear as he sees --

308   CLOSE SHOT - EDELMANN - (PROCESS)

This continues the fourth phase of the transition, during which Edelmann's eyes narrow to slits.

309   CLOSE SHOT - SEIGFRIED - (PROCESS)

He averts his eyes and clucks to the horse again...

310   CLOSE SHOT - EDELMANN - (PROCESS)

The fifth phase of the transition is giving Edelmann's face a pinched, bird-like appearance...

                    EDELMANN
                 (still purring)
         What's the matter, Seigfried...?
         You act as though --

311   CLOSE SHOT - SEIGFRIED - (PROCESS)

Something in Edelmann's voice brings terror into the old
man's heart as:

                    EDELMANN'S VOICE
                    (continues o.s.)
          -- you were afraid...

                    SEIGFRIED
                    (looking straight
                    ahead)
          Oh, no, sir... Why should I be --
          afraid...?

312   CLOSE SHOT - EDELMANN - (PROCESS)

The fifth stage of the transition is intensifying the sadistic, taunting quality in Edelmann's voice.

                    EDELMANN
          Of the night, perhaps...?

The CAMERA PULLS BACK to include Seigfried.

                    SEIGFRIED
          I -- I'm not afraid of the night,
          sir...

                    EDELMANN
          Your hands are trembling, Seig-
          fried...

                    SEIGFRIED
          Are -- are they, sir...?

He snaps the reins again, this time with greater urgency.

                    EDELMANN
          Seigfried...

                    SEIGFRIED
          Yes, sir...?

                    EDELMANN
          I believe I know what you're
          afraid of...

                    SEIGFRIED
          D-do you, sir?

                    EDELMANN
                    (confidentially)
          I believe you're afraid of me...

313   CLOSE SHOT - SEIGFRIED - (PROCESS)

Seigfried swallows again before he finds voice.

                         SEIGFRIED
                  Of -- of you, sir?

                         EDELMANN'S VOICE
                      (o.s.)
                  If you weren't, you'd look at me,
                  Seigfried...

Slowly, the old man turns his head toward him...

314   EDELMANN - (PROCESS)

The sixth stage of the transition has brought malignant,
lustful evil into Edelmann's expression...

315   CLOSE SHOT - SEIGFRIED - (PROCESS)

He stares incredulously, then, turning his eyes ahead,
whips the reins over the horse's flank, sending the animal
into a gallop...

316   CLOSE SHOT EDELMANN AND SEIGFRIED - (PROCESS)

There is more and more of a taunt in Edelmann's voice.

                         EDELMANN
                  You see, you are afraid of me...
                         (as terror holds
                          Seigfried in
                          Stricken silence)
                  -- and you're driving faster and
                  faster so that you can get to the
                  village -- and tell the police
                  what you've seen...
                         (closer)
                  Isn't that it?

                         SEIGFRIED
                  Why -- why should I want -- to
                  tell the police anything...?

                         EDELMANN
                      (fawning)
                  Because you're afraid I'm going
                  to kill you...

317   CLOSE SHOT - EDELMANN - (PROCESS)

The seventh phase of the transition has changed his face
into something which is hardly human. His fingers, now
fully taloned, are joined by webs of flesh.

                         EDELMANN
                      (continued)
             You've seen what's happened to
             your old friend -- and he doesn't
             want anyone but himself to know
             about that...

318   CLOSE SHOT - SEIGFRIED AND EDELMANN - (PROCESS)

                         SEIGFRIED
                      (in terror)
             No, Doctor! I -- I'll never tell...

                         EDELMANN
                      (purring)
             That's right, Seigfried... You
             never will...

His hands reach out and clutch Seigfried's throat. Thrown
off balance, they fall backward into the body of the wagon.

319   MED. LONG PAN SHOT - WAGON

The CAMERA ANGLES with the driverless wagon as it approaches
and passes through an arched opening, the entrance to one
of Visaria's streets...

320   INT. WAGON - CLOSE DOWNWARD ANGLE

-- on Edelmann and Seigfried. During the struggle, Seigfried gets to his feet, dragging Edelmann up with him.
Gripping Edelmann's wrist, Seigfried tears his hands away
from his throat long enogh to cry out:

                         SEIGFRIED
             Help...! Help...!

321   EXT. VISARIA STREET - ENTRANCE TO TAVERN - MED. SHOT

Two or three villagers who have just emerged are reacting
to Seigfried's cry as they look off toward --

322   PAN SHOT - WAGON

The figures of Edelmann and Seigfried are unidentifiable
from the VILLAGER'S ANGLE. As the two men struggle
they fall to the floor of the wagon.

323   GROUP SHOT - VILLAGERS

Several others have come into the scene. Reacting to the
excitement, they run out after the first group, who have
started in pursuit of the wagon,

324   PAN SHOT - WAGON

Edelmann is groveling above Seigfried's body, with his
hands tearing at the old man's throat. A sudden lurch of
the wagon topples Edelmann over and he falls out of the
open end of the wagon, dragging Seigfried with him.

325   CLOSE SHOT - EDELMANN AND SEIGFRIED

They land in the street and roll a couple of times. Edelmann's grip on Seigfried's throat never relaxes...

326   STREET - FULL SHOT

The clatter of the horse's hooves fill the street. Villagers run in from various directions in f.g. As a couple
dash out and stop the horse, Holtz and two of his gendarmes emerge from Police Headquarters. Reacting to the
excitement up the street, they run in that direction.

327   CLOSE SHOT - EDELMANN

He is rising from Seigfried's motionless body, reacting
with alarm as he sees --

328   PAN SHOT - VILLAGERS - (ORIGINAL GROUP)

They are running down the street toward Edelmann.

329   REVERSE SHOT - FROM BEHIND EDELMANN

-- as he turns to look in the opposite direction, reacting to Holtz, his gendarmes, and the other villagers
who are running up the street.

330   CLOSE SHOT - EDELMANN

Seeing that he is being trapped, he runs across the street
in a PAN SHOT into a narrow alley between two buildings.

331   VILLAGERS - (ORIGINAL GROUP)

They change the direction of their pursuit and run after
Edelmann. Several continue down the street toward --

332   MED. GROUP SHOT - NEAR SEIGFRIED

Those of the group who stopped the wagon are now arriving,
together with Holtz and his gendarmes. As the ones who
ran down the street join the group, we hear their CON-
FUSION and AD LIBS, in which we catch significant words:
"Doctor Edelmann's wagon -- " " -- jumped out of the
wagon and ran -- " " -- didn't see who it was -- "

333   COURT AT END OF ALLEY - FULL SHOT

Edelmann runs into view.

334   ENTRANCE TO ALLEY - PAN SHOT - VILLAGERS

The CAMERA PANS them toward the exit into the alley.

335   COURT - FULL SHOT - EDELMANN

Desperately, he runs across the court and disappears into
a narrow space between two buildings.

336   MED. SHOT - ENTRANCE TO COURT

The villagers pour in from the alley and run across the
court in a PAN SHOT toward the only exit in sight, the
one used by Edelmann...

337   MAIN STREET - GROUP SHOT - NEAR SEIGFRIED'S BODY

Holtz is examining Seigfried's body, which is below the
frame line. His two gendarmes are holding the excited
townspeople back as best they can. Steinmuhl enters.

                    HOLTZ
                (to Steinmuhl)
        It's your brother Seigfried...

Steinmuhl, shocked, drops to his knees beside Seigfried's
body.

bv

338   MED. SHOT - FARTHER UP THE STREET

The CAMERA PICKS UP Edelmann and ANGLES with him as he
runs into view from a narrow space between two buildings
and starts up the street in the direction of the arch.

339   GROUP SHOT - AT SEIGFRIED'S BODY

One of the villagers sees the running figure. He ad libs,
"There he goes!" His excitement is contagious. As he
starts out, Holtz, his gendarmes and the other villagers
follow him up the street.

340   PASSAGEWAY BETWEEN BUILDINGS

The first group of pursuers are debouching into the street
with excited ad libs as they pursue Edelmann...

341   ARCH - AT END OF STREET

The CAMERA IS PANNING with Edelmann as he runs toward the
arch.

342   MED. PAN HOT - HOLTZ AND VILLAGERS

They are catching up with the first group of pursuers, who
are running up the street in the direction taken by Edelmann. Their cries and ad libs become louder as they see -

343   LONG SHOT - EDELMANN

He is running toward the trees which lie beyond the arch.

344   PAN SHOT - HOLTZ AND VILLAGERS - NEAR ARCH

The CAMERA ANGLES with them as they exit from the street.

345   MED. LONG SHOT - EDELMANN

He is darting in and out among the trees.

346   PAN SHOT - HOLTZ AND VILLAGERS

The CAMERA PANS with them as they run...

347   AMONG TREES - MED. LONG SHOT

Edelmann's flight through the mist which clings to the
ground gives him the appearance of something which is
floating, rather than running.

348   PAN SHOT - HOLTZ AND VILLAGERS

The shouting villagers scatter among the trees.

349   MED. LONG SHOT - EDELMANN - NEAR GARDEN WALL

The CAMERA SWINGS with him to show that his objective is
the wall, ahead...

350   MED. LONG SHOT - VILLAGERS

Their excited AD LIBS increase as they see --

351   REVERSE - LONG SHOT - TOWARD GARDEN WALL

Edelmann, climbing the vines which cover the wall, disappears over it.

352   PORCH - TALBOT'S ROOM - CLOSE SHOT - TALBOT

He hears the o.s. cries of the villagers and takes a
startled reaction as he sees --

353   MED. ANGLE - FROM PORCH TOWARD WALL

Edelmann drops down from the wall...

354   CLOSE SHOT - EDELMANN ON GROUND

As he drops into view and lies there panting like a hunted
animal, the reverse of the transition changes him into his
normal self.

355   PORCH OF TALBOT'S ROOM - CLOSE SHOT - TALBOT

He is more deeply puzzled as he sees --

356   MED. ANGLE - FROM PROCH ACROSS GARDEN

Getting to his feet, Edelmann runs staggering toward an
entrance into the castle...

357   GROUNDS OF CASTLE - MED. PAN SHOT - HOLTZ AND
        VILLAGERS

        Responding to <u>unintelligible orders</u> shouted by Holtz,
        his gendarmes and the villagers divide into scatter-
        ing groups. Only Steinmuhl continues with Holtz
        toward the castle's entrance.

358   INT. GREAT HALL - MED. SHOT -- NEAR STAIRS

        Edelmann enters. He freezes suddenly as he reacts to-

359   EXT. ENTRANCE OF EDELMANN'S HOME - CLOSE SHOT -
        AT DOORS

        Holtz and Steinmuhl are there. Holtz is banging the
        knocker.

360   INT. GREAT HALL - MED. CLOSE SHOT - EDELMANN

        Edelmann pulls himself together with an effort and
        starts toward the doors.

361   EXT. ENTRANCE OF EDELMANN'S HOME - CLOSE SHOT -
        AT DOORS

        Holtz is banging the knocker more insistently,

363   INT. EDELMANN'S RECEPTION HALL - MED. CLOSE SHOT

        Edelmann, now near the entrance, pauses for a
        moment to collect himself. As he opens the doors
        and sees Holtz and Steinmuhl, he reacts with simulat-
        ed surprise,
                        EDELMANN
                    (with a question-
                    ing inflection)
               Good evening, Inspector,..

                        HOLTZ
               I'm sorry to disturb you, Doctor --

        Nina and Miliza enter in b.g, as Holtz and Steinmuhl
        step inside,

362   GROUP SHOT
                        HOLTZ
                    (continues)
               -- but I'd like to see Mr. Talbot
               and everyone else in the house, at
               once...
                                        CONTINUED

                              EDELMANN
                          (indicating
                           stairway)
            Why certainly, Inspector...
                          (appearing
                           concerned)
            Is something wrong...?

                              HOLTZ
            Something of the gravest consequence...

As he says this, he and Steinmuhl follow Edelmann as
the scene -
                                        WIPES INTO

364   INT. TALBOT'S BEDROOM - FULL GROUP SHOT

Edelmann, Holtz and Steinmuhl enter, followed by
Miliza and Nina, who are obviously disturbed. Edelmann
affects a frowning, annoyed manner. During the scenes
which ensue, Steinmuhl keeps his eyes fixed suspiciously on Talbot.
                              EDELMANN
            Now, Inspector... What is it...?

                              HOLTZ
            Your man Seigfried's been murdered...

                              EDELMANN
                          (appearing stunned)
            Seigfried? Murdered?

                              HOLTZ
            By the person --

365   CLOSE SHOT - TALBOT, MILIZA AND NINA

The two girls are shocked. Talbot, startled by the
thought which has flashed into his mind, is staring
off at Edelmann, reacting sharply to:

                              HOLTZ'S VOICE
                          (continues)
            -- who rode into the village with
            him, tonight... His throat was
            torn open --

366   CLOSE SHOT - HOLTZ, EDELMANN AND STEINMUHL

Holtz turns so that the continuation of his sentence is
in effect addressed to Talbot:
                              HOLTZ
                          (continued)
            -- as though by some enraged animal...

367   FULL GROUP SHOT

All react to the implication. Miliza is terribly concerned.

> TALBOT
> (stoically)
> And naturally you suspect me!

> HOLTZ
> I have good reason to.

> MILIZA
> But he hasn't been out of the house
> for days!

> HOLTZ
> Not to your knowledge perhaps.
> (he questions her coldly)
> Were you with him all of this evening?

> MILIZA
> Up until an hour ago.

> HOLTZ
> The murder was not committed until twenty
> minutes ago -- and within the last five we
> pursued the murderer into these very grounds.

> STEINMUHL
> That's right, almost to this very room.

> MILIZA
> No, no! It's impossible...! Only the
> full moon affects Mr. Talbot -- and the
> moon won't be full again until tomorrow
> night...

> EDELMANN
> Not only that --

368   CLOSE SHOT - TALBOT

He is intent, wondering why Edelmann doesn't mention his
trip into town, with Seigfried. Over this:

> EDELMANN'S VOICE
> -- he's undergone an operation which
> makes physical exertion out of the
> question... Running --

369   CLOSE SHOT - HOLTZ AND EDELMANN

Holtz is beginning to feel that he has been too hasty.

> EDELMANN
> -- even a short distance, much less
> from the village, would have caused
> serious complications -- a cerebral
> hemorrhage --
> (a gesture)
> -- his death...

370   GROUP SHOT

                              HOLTZ
                    Your word is sufficient for me,
                    Doctor...

                              STEINMUHL
                         (virtively)
                    Talbot's the man you want! Are
                    you going to let him talk you
                    out of it!?

                              HOLTZ
                    That's enough, Steinmuhl!
                         (to Edelmann)
                    I apologize, Doctor... But the
                    man who killed his brother is
                    somewhere around here -- and your
                    lives may be in danger... With
                    your permission, I'd like to
                    search the house and grounds...

                              EDELMANN
                    By all means...

As he starts toward the door, Holtz and Steinmuhl follow...

371   CLOSE SHOT - TALBOT, NINA AND MILIZA

The two girls are still resentful of Holtz' implication.
Talbot, looking off toward Edelmann's exit, is deeply
perplexed as the scene --

                                        DISSOLVES TO

372   INT. EDELMANN'S BEDROOM - MED. FULL SHOT

Edelmann is walking up and down the room in a state of
deep agitation as a KNOCK IS HEARD. Collecting himself,
he turns toward the hall door.

                              EDELMANN
                    Yes... Come in...

373   CLOSE SHOT - DOOR

Talbot enters. He looks o.s. for a moment -- then comes
into the room in a PAN SHOT which brings Edelmann into
view. He is obviously controlling himself by great
effort.

                                        CONTINUED

373   CONTINUED

                    TALBOT
          Doctor...

He hesitates, obviously trying to find a way to begin.

                    EDELMANN
          Yes, my boy...

                    TALBOT
          I'd like to talk to you -- about
          what happened, tonight...

                    EDELMANN
                (assuringly)
          Don't let what Holtz said upset
          you...

                    TALBOT
          It isn't that...
                (after a second)
          You were with Seigfried -- when
          he went to the village... I saw
          you --

Edelmann stares at him, shocked to learn that he was seen.

                    TALBOT
                (continued)
          -- when you ran after his wagon
          -- and when you returned...

Edelmann, searching Talbot's face, doesn't answer immediately.

                    EDELMANN
          Why didn't you tell Inspector
          Holtz?

                    TALBOT
          You said nothing.

374   CLOSE SHOT - EDELMANN

He looks off toward Talbot, studying him. His drawn
expression softens with appreciation of Talbot's understanding.

                    EDELMANN
          That was sufficient reason for
          you to keep silent...?

375   CLOSE SHOT - TALBOT AND EDELMANN

                    TALBOT
          You've tried to help me...

                    EDELMANN
          And now, you want to help me?

                    TALBOT
                (sensing tragedy)
          If I can...

                    EDELMANN
                (after a second)
          Because you've suffered the tortures
          I'm going through now, you of all
          people will understand what I'm going
          to say...
                (pause)
          In trying to perform the miracle of
          science, I failed... My blood has
          been contaminated by the blood of
          Dracula...
                (as Talbot stares, shocked)
          My soul and mind have been seized by
          some nameless horror, a lust which robs
          me of all reason and changes me into
          the thing which killed Seigfried, tonight...
                (Talbot is mute with
                sympathy)
          You wish to help me... There's one way
          in which you can... Say nothing to
          Inspector Holtz of what you know...
                (as he sees that Talbot
                misunderstands his reason)
          Not to protect me! Only to give me
          time -- time to do for Nina what I've
          done for you...

Overcome, he grasps the edge of the table for support.

                    EDELMANN
                (continued)
          After that -- this evil thing -- shall
          be destroyed...
                (meaningfully)
          You have my word that it will be, my boy
          -- but if things become too bad -- and
          I fail -- then you -- must do it --
          for me.

He sinks into the chair and buries his face upon his arm.
As the full significance of what Edelmann has said takes
form in Talbot's mind, he rests his hand upon the other
man's shoulder with compassion and understanding of his
tragedy as the scene

                                        DISSOLVES INTO

376   EXT. VISARIA STREET - POLICE HEADQUARTERS - MED. CLOSE
SHOT - NIGHT

As Holtz comes out of the building, a BABBLE OF UNINTEL-
LIGIBLE VOICES IS HEARD o.s. Reacting to this with a
frown, he starts briskly across the street in a PAN SHOT
which brings --

377   BRAHM'S MORTUARY

-- into view. There is a sign in evidence which establishes the nature of the small, chapel-like building
before which is gathered a group of villagers whose
chatter subsides guiltily as they react to Holtz's
approach.

Prominent in f.g. are Steinmuhl, and BRAHMS, the under-
taker. Brahms wears a long, black rubber apron and his
sleeves are rolled up. Holtz enters.

> HOLTZ
> What's going on here...?

> BRAHMS
> I was just on my way to your
> office, Inspector...
> (significantly)
> Have a look at this.

He offers Holtz the article he holds in his hand.

378   CLOSE SHOT - HOLTZ'S HAND

As it comes into the picture, the CAMERA MOVES UP VERY
CLOSE until the article now held by Holtz's fingers is
fully disclosed. It is a smoothly-worn, circular gold
piece, from which hang three or four watch-chain links,
the last of which is stretched but not broken. On the
obverse side is engraved a Gothic University Portal whose
doors are swung wide. On the reverse side, revealed as
Holtz's finger turns the circle over, there are engraved
the words which we hear:

> BRAHMS' VOICE
> (reading)
> 'Doctor Franz Edelmann - Bonn
> University -- Cum Laude -- '

379   GROUP SHOT

All eyes are upon Holtz, watching his reaction as:

CONTINUED

                           BRAHMS
                         (continues)
              It was clenched in Seigfried's
              right hand...

                           STEINMUHL
              And it proves that Doctor Edelmann
              killed him!

Several of the villagers agree with a medley of
OVERLAPPING AD LIBS: " -- he's gone berserk -- " " --
it looks that way to me -- " " -- that's what I think
-- " "Steinmuhl's right -- " " -- Edelmann's the
murderer -- "

                           HOLTZ
                         (furiously)
              Be quiet!
                         (to Steinmuhl,
                          as the ad libs
                          subside)
              You don't know what this means
              and neither do I! But it's some-
              thing for the police to handle,
              not you! Is that clear!?

                           STEINMUHL
                         (belligerently)
              It's clear that Doctor Edelmann
              killed my brother.

                           HOLTZ
              Last night you thought it was
              Talbot! Tonight you say it's a
              man whom all of us have known
              and trusted for years! You're
              worse than a gossiping old woman!
                         (to others)
              Go home -- all of you!

As he exits abruptly, the CAMERA MOVES UP CLOSER to
Steinmuhl. Like any other braggart-extrovert, he
tries now to justify his position by haranguing his
listeners.

                           STEINMUHL
              Something's going on at Doctor
              Edelmann's, I tell you! What
              about that business of wanting
              to explore the cave!? Why was
              he in such a hurry to get down
              there -- then didn't come back!?
              When I asked Seigfried, he said
              it was the Doctor's business!
                         (cont'd)

                              STEINMUHL (cont'd)
              But he knew what was going on -
              and that's why Doctor Edelmann
              killed him! And what does Holtz
              have to say about it?
                      (aping Holtz)
              'This is something for the police
              to handle...'
                      (himself again)
              It's something for us to handle
              -- unless we all want to be mur-
              dered!

Heads wag and there are <u>angry mutterings</u> from his
listeners as the scene -

                                      DISSOLVES INTO

380   EXT. EDELMANN'S GARDEN - TERRACE - MED. CLOSE SHOT -
       NEAR FRENCH WINDOW

       Lights are burning in the Great Hall as Edelmann and
       Talbot, a few feet ahead of Miliza and Nina, come out
       onto the terrace. The CAMERA PANS WITH them so that
       when Talbot pauses at the low step to the garden path,
       his and Edelmann's backs are to the Camera and the
       CHANGING ANGLE shows the distant horizon over the
       garden wall. Small, fleecy, low-lying clouds are being
       touched by the unseen moon's silvering light.

381   CLOSE SHOT - TALBOT AND EDELMANN

       Nina and Miliza have stopped behind them. Edelmann,
       whose expression reflects the turmoil of his own
       problem, is checking any outward display of his real
       emotions. Talbot's face is drawn, haggard from the
       strain of waiting and hoping -- and doubting.

                              TALBOT
              Suppose that all you've done --
              fails...?

       Miliza steps impulsively to his side and links her
       hand upon his arm.

                              EDELMANN
                      (assuringly)
              The physical causes no longer
              exist...
                      (firmly)
              The rest is up to you... Put
              fear out of your mind...Confront
              this moment with the belief that
              the past is over with, and that a
              new life lies ahead...

                                      CONTINUED

381   CONTINUED

Talbot closes his eyes, as though to lock out the
fears which besiege him.

                    NINA
                (encouragingly)
        A new life does lie ahead!

                    MILIZA
        Have faith, Larry!

Talbot looks at her for a moment, then puts her hand
gently away.

                    TALBOT
        Stay here... all of you...,

                    MILIZA
        No, Larry! I want to be with
        you!

                    TALBOT
        Please... Stay here... until
        we're certain...

He exits abruptly, Miliza makes a move to follow.
Nina, stepping quickly to her side, restrains her.

382   CLOSE SHOT - TALBOT

The CAMERA, MOVING AHEAD of him, is taking him
farther and farther from those on the terrace.

383   CLOSE SHOT - NINA AND MILIZA

-- in a ANGLE WHICH INCLUDES Edelmann, a couple
of steps behind them. Looking off toward Talbot,
he is unconsciously flexing his fingers -- an
indication of the transition to come upon him soon.
Miliza and Nina, in the grip of suspenseful emotions,
are looking off toward --

384   TALBOT

-- who, now some distance away from the terrace, pauses
in a CLOSE SHOT. Struggling to overcome fear almost
beyond his strength to endure, he stares fixedly toward
--

385   THE GARDEN WALL

-- beyond which the moon is beginning to rise.

386   CLOSE SHOT — TALBOT

He is taut in every muscle as the moonlight begins to
bathe his face...

387   CLOSE SHOT — NINA AND MILIZA

-- in an ANGLE which does not show Edelmann. The girls
are breathless as they look off toward Talbot.

388   CLOSE SHOT — TALBOT

He clenches his hands, forcing himself to look off toward -

389   THE GARDEN WALL

-- over which more than half the moon is now visible.

390   CLOSE SHOT — TALBOT

Fear chills his heart as his face becomes more fully
illumined by the moonlight.

391   CLOSE SHOT — MILIZA AND NINA

Miliza takes a step forward, then stops, checking an almost
irresistible desire to go to Talbot...

392   CLOSE SHOT — TALBOT

He is trembling now as he sees --

393   MED. SHOT — ANGLING FROM BEHIND TALBOT

-- over the garden wall as the tangent of the moon's
apparent contact with the horizon separates and leaves
it round and full against the sky.

394   REVERSE CLOSE SHOT — TALBOT

His face is fully illumined. Now, he brings his arms
slowly upward, lowering his gaze to look at his hands.
As he stares at them and sees no evidence of the hairy
growth which always accompanied the change, the realization that he is free begins to appear in his eyes.

ae

395   CLOSE SHOT - MILIZA

Unable to tell from Talbot's manner whether or not he has conquered, Miliza watches for seconds which to her seem like eternities of waiting...

396   LONG SHOT - FROM TERRACE - IN THE GARDEN

Talbot, silhouetted against the moon, now raises his arms toward it in a moment of exultation and defiance.

397   CLOSE SHOT - MILIZA

A surge of emotions carries her from the terrace in a PAN SHOT which brings Talbot into view.

398   CLOSE SHOT - NINA

There is tender understanding in her eyes as she looks off toward -

399   MED. CLOSE SHOT - TALBOT AND MILIZA

Reaching Talbot, Miliza stands beside him, clinging to his arm, smiling now as she sees that the look of haunting terror has disappeared from his face. Talbot, still trying to realize that he is free, sinks onto the bench beside which he and Miliza stand and buries his head against the comforting softness of her while she, too full of happiness for utterance, strokes his hair.

400   CLOSE SHOT - NINA

A smile transfigures her face as she turns to where Edelmann was standing.

                    NINA
          Doctor! It's wonderful...

She stops, silenced by what the CAMERA REVEALS as it PULLS BACK INTO A LARGER SHOT. Edelmann has disappeared. Unable to understand why he should have left without even a word, Nina looks off toward Miliza and Talbot for a second, then, deeply worried, exits into the Great Hall...

401   TALBOT AND MILIZA - CLOSE SHOT

Their faces, bathed in the Moonlight, are radiant.

CONTINUED

401   CONTINUED

                         TALBOT
              The night is beautiful...

                         MILIZA
                        (softly)
              I'm so happy for you Larry...

        She rests her head against his shoulder.

402   EXT. VISARIA STREET - FULL SHOT

        -- ANGLING THROUGH the archway. A hundred or more vil-
        lagers, led by Steinmuhl and Brahms, are milling through
        the archway onto the road... Many of them are armed with
        whatever they found handy when incited into action.

403   INT. SURGERY, LABORATORY - CLOSE SHOT - NINA - AT DOOR

        Sounds of the apparatus are heard as the door opens and
        Nina enters, pausing when just within the room to look
        o.s. as she sees -

404   MED. CLOSE SHOT - EDELMANN - FROM NINA'S ANGLE

        The straps which bound the Monster to the table have been
        unfastened. Edelmann, turning the voltage control higher,
        talks to the Monster as would a mother encouraging her
        child to try its first steps.

                         EDELMANN
              Now... Now!

        Slowly, the Monster begins to raise his ponderous torso.

                         EDELMANN
              That's it, that's it!

        As he continues to raise the voltage, the Monster's huge
        hands grip the edges of the table and he uses his arms
        as levers to lift his body slowly to a sitting position.

405   CLOSE SHOT - NINA

        Nina leaves the door impulsively in a PAN SHOT which
        brings Edelmann again into view, but in an ANGLE which
        still conceals his face from her.

406   REVERSE SHOT - ANGLING OVER EDELMANN AND THE MONSTER

-- as Nina approaches and stops near the table. She
stares spellbound at the Monster, who is now swinging
himself to a swaying, standing position beside Edelmann,
whose back is still to Nina so that she cannot as yet
see his face. Edelmann's voice is soothing as he talks
to the Monster.

                    EDELMANN
          They tried to kill you... but they
          couldn't... Frankenstein gave you
          eternal life -- power, which time
          cannot destroy -- the secret of
          immortality, which will soon be
          mine --
                    (patting the Mon-
                     ster's arm)
          I'll make you strong -- stronger
          than you've ever been -- I'll give
          you the strength of a hundred men...

                    NINA
          No Doctor Edelmann -- no! You
          promised that --

Startled by her voice, Edelmann whirls to face her.

                    EDELMANN
          What are you doing here!?

                    NINA
          Why, I --

The words freeze on her lips as she reacts with shocked
horror to the change in Edelmann.

                    EDELMANN
                    (speaking softly)
          You were spying on me, weren't
          you...?

As he takes a step forward, Nina backs away, staring.
Edelmann's voice now becomes soothing.

                    EDELMANN
          You shouldn't have done that, Nina...
          I don't like people who see what
          they're not supposed to see...
                    (advancing)

407   CLOSE SHOT - NINA

Stark disbelief is in her eyes as she continues to back
slowly away...

408   CLOSE SHOT - EDELMANN

His face is a distorted smile as he moves CLOSER AND
CLOSER TO THE CAMERA.

409   EXT. ENTRANCE EDELMANN'S HOME - MED. GROUP SHOT

Holtz and two of his gendarmes are there. Holtz is banging the knocker imperatively.

410   INT. RECEPTION HALL - MED. SHOT

Sounds of the high-frequency apparatus are heard o.s. as
Talbot and Miliza, reacting to the continued knocking,
enter from the garden. Miliza opens the door.

                         MILIZA
               Yes, Inspector...?

Holtz and his men brush past her into the hall, leaving
the door open.

                         HOLTZ
               I want to see Doctor Edelmann, at
               once...

Miliza and Talbot, worried by Holtz's brusque manner,
exchange glances, just as a PIERCING SCREAM from Nina
is HEARD. Reacting as one when this is followed by
another and more chilling scream, the group, led by
Holtz, run in a PAN SHOT into the Great Hall toward the
laboratory...

411   EXT. GROUNDS OF EDELMANN'S ESTATE - FULL SHOT

The villagers, led by Steinmuhl and Brahms, are pouring
through the gates...

412   INT. SURGERY, LABORATORY - MED. CLOSE SHOT - DOOR

Holtz and his two men enter, followed closely by Talbot
and Miliza. All stand frozen, appalled into silence by
what they see -

413   MED. FULL SHOT

Edelmann, beside whom stands the Monster, has his back
to the Camera so that his body conceals the bestiality
of his actions. He is obviously strangling Nina, who
has already become limp in his hands. He flings her
away from him...

414   GROUP SHOT - TALBOT, MILIZA, ET AL

A cry chokes in Miliza's throat. She and Talbot, horror-
stricken, run out toward Nina.

                    HOLTZ
          The Frankenstein Monster...!

He draws his pistol. His men follow his lead as they
rush into the room...

415   CLOSE SHOT - NINA

Talbot and Miliza kneel beside her and support her lifeless body in their arms.

416   MED. SHOT - EDELMANN AND MONSTER

Holtz and his men, who are reaching f.g. just as Edelmann
turns to face them, are stopped short as they react to
the change they see in Edelmann. Holtz and his men stare
with amazed disbelief.

                    GENDARME
          That's him! He's the one I saw
          the night Seigfried was murdered!

                    HOLTZ
                  (aghast)
          Doctor! Doctor Edelmann!

                    EDELMANN
          Yes, Holtz! Doctor Edelmann!

                    HOLTZ
          Take him!

As he starts toward Edelmann, the Monster steps protect-
ingly between them, roaring with rage. One of the
gendarmes fires his pistol point-blank into his chest.
Diverted from Holtz for an instant, the Monster turns
upon the two men, knocking them aside with his outflung
arms. During this, the cables tear away from the
electrodes in his neck and short-circuit with a spectacular flash...

417   CLOSE SHOT - MILIZA, TALBOT AND NINA

Talbot, reacting as he looks o.s., springs to his feet and
runs out toward --

418   MED. CLOSE SHOT - EDELMANN, MONSTER, ET AL

Holtz and Edelmann are struggling. As Talbot rushes in
and intervenes in an effort to help Holtz, the monster
flings him violently away in a PAN SHOT which holds on
Talbot until he falls across a table, dazed for a few
seconds by the monster's blow. Miliza, seen in the b.g.,
leaves Nina and runs toward Talbot.

419   MED. CLOSE - EDELMANN, MONSTER, ET AL

Edelmann's expression is one of distorted passion as he
watches the monster spin Holtz away from him with a mighty
sweep of his arm. As Holtz reels backward, he drops his
pistol.

420   MED. CLOSE - HIGH-FREQUENCY SWITCHBOARD

Holtz reels backward into the scene. As he lands against
the exposed high-voltage switches, the apparatus short-
circuits with a display of electrical effects which
electrocute him. (During the ensuing intimate scenes
between Talbot and Edelmann, the gendarmes get to their
feet and continue an AD LIB conflict with the monster.)

421   CLOSE SHOT - EDELMANN

H e turns now to look off toward --

422   CLOSE SHOT - TALBOT AND MILIZA

Talbot, recovered, is looking off scene, reacting as he
sees --

423   CLOSE SHOT - EDELMANN

He picks up a heavy, menacing piece of apparatus and walks
slowly toward Talbot and Miliza.

                    EDELMANN
          You broke your promise to me,
          Talbot... You told the police...

424   MED. GROUP SHOT - TALBOT, MILIZA AND EDELMANN

Miliza, paralyzed by fear, stifles a scream. Talbot,
putting himself between her and Edelmann, makes a dash
for Holtz' pistol.

425   CLOSE SHOT - EDELMANN

He turns quickly and starts toward Talbot, snarling.

426   CLOSE SHOT - TALBOT

He picks up the pistol and turns quickly to confront
Edelmann.

427   CLOSE SHOT - EDELMANN

Advancing slowly, he has his weapon upraised, ready to
kill...

428   CLOSE SHOT - TALBOT

Knowing what he must do, he is sick at heart.

                    TALBOT
          Doctor! Doctor Edelmann...!

429   CLOSE SHOT - EDELMANN

Heedless of the warning plea in Talbot's voice, he
continues to advance.

430   CLOSE SHOT - TALBOT

Steeling himself to the act, he raises the pistol...

431   CLOSE SHOT - EDELMANN

He is closer to Talbot than before.

432   CLOSE SHOT - TALBOT

He fires...

433   CLOSE SHOT - EDELMANN

The heavy iron weapon drops from his hands as he crumples
to the floor.

434   CLOSE SHOT - MILIZA

Miliza, shocked, covers her eyes and turns away.

435   CLOSE SHOT - TALBOT

He is staring down at Edelmann's body, numbed for the
moment by the realization of what he has had to do.

436   MED. SHOT - MONSTER AND GENDARMES

The continued conflict has ended in defeat for the
gendarmes and the monster is now starting toward Talbot.

437   CLOSE SHOT - MONSTER

He stops in close f.g. looking down at --

438   CLOSE SHOT - EDELMANN ON FLOOR

A DISSOLVE transmutes his bestial expression into that of
the kindly Doctor Edelmann.

439   CLOSE SHOT - MONSTER.

He lets loose a roar of rage and starts menacingly toward
Talbot.

440   CLOSE SHOT - MILIZA

Looking o.s., she cries a warning.

                    MILIZA
          Larry !

She rushes out toward him.

441   CLOSE SHOT - TALBOT

Just as Talbot turns, Miliza runs into scene. The monster
brushes her away with a backhand sweep of his arm.

442   CLOSE SHOT - MILIZA

The CAMERA PANS with her until she falls to the floor and
lies there, unconscious.

443   CLOSE SHOT - TALBOT AND MONSTER

As the monster advances, Talbot fires his pistol and falls
back a step...

444   EXT. ENTRANCE EDELMANN'S HOME - FULL SHOT

The shouting villagers are crowding through the open
doorway...

445   INT. SURGERY, LABORATORY - MILIZA, STEINMUHL, TALBOT AND
MONSTER

As Talbot fires his pistol again, the monster seizes him
and flings him away with a bellow of fury.

446   CLOSE SHOT - TALBOT

The CAMERA PANS with him as he reels backward into scene
and falls to the floor.

447   CLOSE SHOT - MONSTER

He starts toward Talbot, flinging things out of his way
as he advances.

448   MEDIUM CLOSE - ENTRANCE FROM HALL

Steinmuhl and the villagers rush into the room, frozen
near the entrance for a moment by what they see.

449   CLOSE SHOT - TALBOT

As he gets to his feet, he sees the villagers and shouts:

                    TALBOT
          Get out! It's the Frankenstein
          Monster!...

450   MED. GROUP - ENTRANCE FROM HALL

We hear a medley of excited AD LIBS: "The Frankenstein
Monster!" -- "Edelmann brought him back to life!" -- Some
of the more timid turn and flee. Others charge toward
the monster, throwing whatever they find handy...

451   CLOSE SHOT - MONSTER

He turns and starts savagely toward the villagers.

452   CLOSE SHOT - TALBOT

The CAMERA IS PANNING with him as he moves toward the
monster and the villagers.

                                        CONTINUED

452   CONTINUED

                              TALBOT
              Get out ! Get out !

        Pausing near a large, wheeled cabinet, Talbot seizes it
        impulsively and gives it a shove toward the Monster...

453   MED. CLOSE - MONSTER

        The cabinet crashes into him and topples over, spilling
        its bottles to the floor. As the chemicals combine, there
        is an explosion which envelopes the Monster from head to
        feet in a winding sheet of flame.

454   GROUP SHOT - VILLAGERS

        Panic stricken by the explosion and the imminent fire,
        they start to flee...

455   CLOSE SHOT - MONSTER (STOCK)

        As the flames begin to rise all around him.

456   CLOSE SHOT - MILIZA

        Talbot rushes into scene and starts to lift her in his
        arms.

457   CLOSE SHOT - MONSTER (STOCK)

        Seen through the flames, he starts to go berserk.

458   CLOSE SHOT - BASE OF CEILING'S SUPPORT

        Syrupy streams of liquids pouring from two of the large
        bottles, are creeping over the floor toward each other.
        As they meet, there is a violent chemical reaction --
        heavy smoke, followed by a deafening explosion. As the
        supporting column gives way, a new burst of flames leap
        upward.

459   FULL SHOT

        As the flames in the background leap higher and debris
        begins to fall, the last of the fleeing villagers are
        exiting. As Talbot reaches f.g. carrying Miliza in his
        arms, there comes the SOUND and the FLASH from another
        explosion.

gs   "DESTINY" - Changes 9/20/45

460   CLOSE SHOT - MONSTER (STOCK)

He is terrorized and trying desperately to find some way out of this inferno.

461   EXT. - ANGLING INTO LABORATORY THROUGH WINDOW (STOCK)

The frenzied Monster is fighting the flames as a large beam crashes downward from above, and knocks him OUT OF SCENE.

462   INT. SURGERY, LABORATORY - MED. SHOT

The Monster falls and slides toward Edelmann's body. As the crazed creature clings to Edelmann's body, as though seeking help from the one who befriended him, the portion of the floor upon which they lie begins to sag and gives way, and falls out of sight. The Monster drags Edelmann's body along with him.

463   DOWNWARD ANGLE - INTO PIT

Linked together in death, they drop into the yawning maw, followed by an avalanche of masonry and burning beams. Timbers drop down upon them, becoming a consuming pyre which envelops them as the scene·

DISSOLVES INTO

464   EXT. EDELMANN'S GARDEN - MED. REVERSE SHOT - TALBOT AND MILIZA

They are two silhouetted figures, walking hand in hand into the light of the full moon which shines beyond them.

FADE OUT

THE END

* * *

* *

*

www.ingramcontent.com/pod-product-compliance
Lightning Source LLC
Chambersburg PA
CBHW050354110426
42812CB00008B/2457